QStory

Raising Our Voices:
Stories from the LGBTQ Community

Edited by Nicci Robinson
2021

QStory

Raising Our Voices: Stories from the LGBTQ Community

Cataloguing information
ISBN: 979-8-594992-72-6

Credits

Editor: Nicci Robinson
Cover Design: Nicci Robinson, Global Wordsmiths
Production Design: Global Wordsmiths

Dedication

To all those waiting for their stories to be told.
With thanks to Global Wordsmiths
for helping us tell ours.

Introduction

We believe in the power of stories. They help us to understand ourselves and the world, to connect, build communities, and to see who we might become. But for many LGBTQIA people, stories reflecting our diverse realities have been missing for much of our lives.

For our generation, government legislation meant queer stories were hidden. We were both toddlers when Section 28 was first brought in by the Conservative party. It dictated that local authorities "shall not intentionally promote homosexuality or publish material with the intention of promoting homosexuality." Not only did our sex and relationships education consequently ignore the existence of LGBTQIA people, but our local libraries were forbidden from carrying books or films which contained gay or lesbian themes.

As two bookish teens trying to understand our sexualities and figure out our place in the world, we took this lack of queer stories to heart. At the time, we weren't aware of Section 28's existence and didn't know why we couldn't find them. The act wasn't repealed until we were in our late teens, and its impact on queer people of our generation can't be overstated. Many of us, along with those of previous generations, grew up with no opportunity to explore or understand our queerness. We had no idea that it was okay to be ourselves.

These days, things are much better although of course, nowhere near perfect. In 2009, then Prime Minister, David Cameron, finally apologised for Section 28 and the harm it caused to our community (a major turnaround considering he voted against its repeal in 2003). But recently there have been worrying trends, particularly focusing on the transgender members of our community, where people are again questioning whether children should have access to education about LGBTQIA issues that validate our identities in the name of "protecting" them. We know that lack of access to queer material didn't protect us, quite the opposite in fact. We're passionate about ensuring that, unlike us, future generations grow up seeing themselves in stories and have words for their experiences.

We put together this project to give queer people the opportunity to tell their stories, fictional or otherwise, and to give others the chance to read them. The stories collected in this anthology were written during a series of writing workshops run by Global Wordsmiths, which were open to all local LGBTQIA people. Some of the participants had prior experience of creative writing, some had none. Some have dreams of becoming professional writers, some simply enjoyed trying their hand at something new. All of their stories are powerful and inspiring.

We have loved working with this fabulous group and are proud of their wonderful words. We hope you enjoy and take pride in their stories too.

Cat and Liz,
Organisers, QStory Northampton

CONTENTS

Ardha Chandrasana: Bending So I Didn't Break
by Katie Kieran Port   1

The Taxi Driver
by Briony Hastings   15

Red Lipstick
by Claire Deacon   31

Boxed In and Coming Out
by Phoebe Gracey   37

Dance of the Bees
by A.J. Herbert   45

Out at Last
by C.W. Sinclair   57

Moon Children
by Eleanor Holloway   69

Faith and Pride
by Abigail James   85

Ardha Chandrasana: Bending So I Didn't Break

by Katie Kieran Port

Hope is always out there.

It all started toward the end of 2014, a couple of years after losing my dad and my good friend, JD, to cancer, and I felt like I needed to change myself in order to fit in with my circle of friends. I was absolutely aching with so much anxiety and trauma.

My fears were drowning me, my self-esteem had been shattered, and I would often wake with a deep, engulfing feeling of panic. My heart ached with such a profound loss that I felt sure it might break and stop working at any moment. My insecurities had me feeling not good enough or worthy of the love I wanted or the life I desired. The winter, cold weather, and lack of light had always impacted my mood and distorted my reality, but my grieving tripled its effects. Over the years, I'd been in unhealthy relationships, ones with people who didn't just blow out the candle in my soul, they'd been stealing them. I came to depend on others for the light I craved. My spirit had broken into a jigsaw I was unable to piece back together, not because of one person or one experience, just like it's not one bag that breaks the camel's back, but the accumulative effect of *everything*.

My anxiety was physically painful, a dull ache, as cold as ice, which gripped my whole body. My muscles would clench themselves, as if trying to protect me from feeling so frozen. And it fucking hurt. It hurt to not feel worthy, not to be enough, not to be *seen*. Despite me rising up again and again to face the challenges thrown in front of me, I was always two steps behind. My heart ached and I spiralled, utterly lost. I suddenly realized that over the years, I'd been shrinking myself inside to please others. I'd been filling myself with sadness and carrying around so many insecurities. And in this moment, I didn't know how to be myself again. I didn't have the strength to love myself enough to take those steps, towards embracing being my whole authentic self.

However, throughout the intensity and desperation of my emotions, I knew that only *I* could change things. *I* had to get, or perhaps just feel, stronger to break this unhealthy cycle of caring too much about what others think. And most importantly, I needed to address the voice within that echoed everything threatening to destroy me.

That voice needed to shut up too!

I had only been diagnosed with Asperger's less than six months before. And I remember the feeling of huge relief that came with this new knowledge, because suddenly my life made a lot more sense: the anxiety that I wore every day, the confusion in my heart, when friends and loved ones said or did something that utterly confused me. And how, from the moment I came out as being queer, I knew the typical gay scene didn't fit me or my personality. The rainbow bars and clubs with their loud music vibrated inside of me like an audio version of a panic attack, and the flashing lights were overstimulating and made me dizzy. I also didn't drink alcohol. I've never quite liked the taste, but your twenties is like a rite of passage through downing pint after pint and shot after shot. I stood out like a sore thumb with my pint…of water, standing on the side lines as everyone was losing their shit and somehow having fun. There had to be something else out there for us young, non-clubbing type queers I thought. I can't be the only one, although in my small town, I certainly felt like it.

I had yet to meet anyone quite like me, who shared my passion for curiosity, adventure, and a vision for an artistic queer scene. And so slowly, and with the "help" of others' criticisms, I began to shrink myself. My friends at the time were trying to be helpful by encouraging me to become more like them. I felt under pressure to conform to mainstream expectations by going out to those noisy clubs and toning down the way I dressed, which was an expression of my queer, creative self. My eager wings, searching for something more *me* with their colourful feathers, were clearly too bright for those around me to appreciate. Instead they caused me trouble, they needed taming and I was encouraged to clip them. "It's for your own good," those friends would say. "It will stop you standing out so much."

I couldn't change who I was, but maybe if I coloured myself black and white instead, I would stop standing out so much and *look* like I fit in.

But now years later, my black and white wings were beginning to rattle against that old and unhelpful cage. I could hear the voices of my loved ones, especially my dad, in my head, saying, "How dare you dull yourself to fit in?" My family had always encouraged me to be myself, with pride.

So my Asperger's diagnosis meant that I wasn't a misfit in society or an overthinker, and neither was I being too sensitive. Instead, I'm a neurodiverse person navigating my way through a neurotypical world. And I just hadn't found the people who shared my passion and curiosity for something outside the mainstream. The world outside of that cage was much bigger and brighter. And now was my time to fly.

I had a few fantastic friends. And my family were amazing, especially my mum who has been extremely supportive. My mum is a real Mama Bear and has always fought in my corner with her feisty love and compassion.

It was a cold and wet winter evening. I was walking home with KJ, a close friend of mine, after attending a poetry event. I confided in her about my anxiety and how I felt lost, and she said she'd suffered a similar thing and had turned to yoga one-to-ones. Over time she began to feel less overwhelmed. I didn't really know anything about the ancient art and benefits of yoga, but my curiosity awoke and I was intrigued. I came across a poster advertising "Yoga with Ali" at Open Stage, a performing arts school, and I began toying with the idea of giving it a go. What did I have to lose?

I was accustomed to attending things by myself, but this particular winter's night in December was different. I wasn't just doing something by myself, I was *choosing* to try something new. And new can feel daunting for anyone, but more especially so when you're on the autistic spectrum. Our anxiety around change and uncertainty can see us sticking to the already known and to play safe. Fortunately though, and ever the paradox, *my* personality also craves excitement, adventure, and movement.

My walk up that steep road leading to the Open Stage building was, unbeknown to me at the time, the beginning of something special. And as I walked up the hill that felt more like a mountain on many levels, dragging my heavy feet in my new orange and black trainers, my mind was both reminding me how brave I was in my black leather, studded jacket (the one I always donned for confidence) whilst also asking me what the hell I was doing. *Why do you believe yoga is going to help you?* My stomach was tied in knots and it took a great deal of psyching myself up, but I took the plunge that evening into the unknown and embraced my curiosity.

I arrived early and as I stood outside the huge red doors, I began taking deep breaths whilst watching cars pass me by. They brought me back to the moment when they occasionally beeped their horns at one another. I was determined not to let my butterflies—more like bats—get the better of me, and I gently pulled open one of the wooden doors to enter. Open Stage Performing Arts Company is exactly that, and as I opened that beautiful and brightly coloured door, I was confronted with a huge hall with a stage.

My first yoga class started out as being a one-to-one yoga lesson, because nobody else showed up that night; it *was* two weeks before Christmas. A time when most people are busy with their work Christmas social or making the most of later opening times to finalise their shopping. Two things that I happily avoided. On reflection, it was exactly what I needed as I tended to shrink in group settings, and this felt a little less overwhelming. Almost like that person in school, who blends in and becomes part of the wallpaper, that person who is so quiet, you forget they were there in class with you at all.

I sat down on a glazed wooden bench, which was pushed up against the large windows of the hall, and looked out over a beautiful garden. I started fiddling with the zip of my yoga bag. I'd messaged Ali the night before to express my interest and about my possible attendance this evening. Ali walked over to me, after bringing in her gigantic bag of yoga bricks and mats from her car, and greeted me with what I now know is her huge, trademark smile, and she quickly put some of my anxieties at ease. Ali asked me whether I'd ever done any type of yoga before or if I knew much about it. I explained that I hadn't, that this was my first time, and I didn't really know anything about yoga other than what I'd seen on Instagram, where the people and their poses and body shapes didn't look like me or my full and curvy body. However I'm hypermobile and I was a gymnastic champion as a child, so I was confident that I could make some impressive shapes with my body. But mostly I was there to learn some new tools to de-mobilize the constant anxiety that I was feeling, and which I'd been feeling for too long. Ali listened, reassured me, and said that there was a whole lot more to yoga than the exaggerated poses on Instagram. The art of breathing and breath work was vital too, especially for anxiety. Her words gave me my first glimmer of hope.

My hands were sweaty as I pulled my orange yoga mat out of my bag. I'd brought my own mat as I like to plan ahead and feel prepared, and my favourite colour is orange. I love warm colours, and orange reminds me of my spiritual practices, Buddhism and meditation, something which I'd been doing for over a decade at this point. I unrolled it and threw it out flat upon the hard wooden floor of the hall before me. We began with first laying on my mat and bringing ourselves into the present, encouraging me to leave my anxieties at the door. My first lesson was similar to my Buddhist practices - mindfulness and learning to be present. Ali encouraged me to feel the ground beneath me and only be in this moment, before she went into sun salutations. This is a practice in yoga that incorporates a sequence of twelve gracefully linked asanas in sequences, like moving around a sun, and it was my first experience of downward facing dog and planking.

Halfway through the class I had an anxiety attack. My past experiences had taught me that when I had anxiety attacks in public, the people around me tended to panic in response, which further fuels my own anxiety. But Ali was different, she gave me water and managed to settle me down quickly. I felt she genuinely understood and cared. I enjoyed my first lesson and felt motivated to go back. Although I didn't really know Ali and how yoga was really going to help me, my instincts told me to trust the universe, have faith in myself, and to return.

Which of course, I did. I kept up my yoga lessons, and it's been nearly six years of grateful practice now.

Yoga is actually the first and longest hobby that I've ever stuck to when it comes to things that interest me. Perhaps because, nearly six years on, I'm aware it's because you're constantly learning and discovering new things. My sustained yoga practice is something I still find incredible. I celebrated my first year of yoga, especially the body confidence it taught me, with a special body piercing.

I was very fortunate to begin yoga one-to-ones with Ali the following winter in 2015. In that year I'd been building up my trust with Ali, as well as my practice. Those yoga classes became my weekly therapy sessions where I thrived, as I took my yoga practice and understanding further. It also let another person begin to see me, *really see me*, as each layer of shame, loneliness, and the hidden pain of feeling different, began to peel away one at a time. And the whole time, this was being reinforced with self-love, compassion, acceptance, authenticity, and the ownership of the beauty of being myself.

These lessons led to my everyday yoga tools becoming more personal with the introduction of Mr Socks, my loving, sweet, and sassy cat, whose black and white markings resemble a tuxedo complete with two white socks. Mr Socks came to live with me a year before my dad passed away and I often felt like he was the only soul who genuinely knew me and accepted everything I was. Mr Socks and his loyalty became my grounding tool for love and comfort. And whenever my anxiety felt too overwhelming, Ali would use Mr Socks to bring me back again.

The importance of being able to understand the tactile sensory difficulties I face every day and my body's reactions to these sensations was a learning curve too. For example, I was hypersensitive to light touch, which would cause my skin to feel itchy when I wore certain fabrics. If someone were to gently brush my skin, it felt like they were dragging their nails down a chalkboard and it made my skin crawl. However, I was also hyposensitive to deep pressure, which meant that having a weighted blanket placed on my body was like floating on a cosy dream cloud. Deep pressure is soothing for me but is also the reason why I often don't notice the big, shining, purple bruises forming on my arms after clumsily walking into another door handle. So yoga has been important to help me make sense of and understand these sensory differences. And it was definitely something better explored one to one, as making certain shapes in yoga can sometimes bring up emotions.

I felt unsettled at first during opening heart poses in the weekly group class. I recall placing one of Ali's purple yoga bricks under my chest, laying on my mat whilst my arms were spread wide open, and I cried, which made me feel silly. Why was I crying? I loved yoga. And I didn't even feel low that day... I blamed my hormones. But then it happened again the following week. I didn't understand why I would suddenly feel this way so when those feelings began to surface in the group class, I would take some breaths and sit on my mat to gather myself and my thoughts while the rest of the class continued.

So at my next one-to-one, I explained to Ali that whenever we attempted any heart open poses, I felt a shift happening, and the anxiety from my chest began to slowly move up into my throat, especially upon stretching into half-moon pose. This pose not only involves me opening my heart out but doing so while standing and balancing using only half of my body, which is particularly challenging on focus and self-confidence.

"I can't breathe, and I feel like something is choking me," I would explain to Ali with tears running down my cheeks as I started to massage my tight throat. "I'm scared. I'm scared I'm going to cry and break down."

Those feelings and thoughts of being too much, feeling too much, and being oversensitive reared their ugly heads. I was worried about Ali seeing me and her running away, rejecting me for showing too much emotion. Instead she sat with me and my discomfort and calmly encouraged me to cry, tenderly explaining that not only wasn't there any *shame* in crying, but it was also healthy to shed tears.

Ali's words took me aback. I knew deep down that they were true but showing my feelings like this had always caused people to feel uncomfortable. I really hoped that Ali and her kindness were real. She wasn't like anyone else. I kept waiting for her to see something unacceptable in me and reject me, but it hadn't happened. I let the tears fall, with both relief and hope.

We attempted a sequence of warrior poses again, and as my tears fell whilst opening my heart, I raised up my arm, kicked out the side of my leg into a half moon pose, and held it with strength. The anxiety in my throat poured out and the wings of those butterflies just tickled my throat as they flew out.

The half moon pose has now become my go-to pose to show myself and my anxieties that I'm stronger than my fear.

It didn't matter how much anxiety Ali saw in our one-to-one lessons or how many times she witnessed me having a meltdown when I was feeling discouraged by yet another fork in the road. With her tender voice and gentle compassion, she would remind me of my courage and tenacity and encouraged me to see this for myself. Ali empowered me to change my dialogue with fear, anxiety, and social pressures by viewing them from another perspective.

"Despite your everyday anxieties and the deck of cards that you've been dealt, rain or shine, you still *choose* to show up every week to your practice, and not because you *have* to, but because you *want* to," she said.

Ali motivated me to wear my story like a badge on my favourite black leather jacket. To own my story and all of its colourful chapters and to see that no page, however smudged it may look, needed erasing. What may look like imperfection to one will be a tale of beauty and courage to another. Our paths are rarely straightforward and at times require us backstepping for a moment to reposition ourselves and find a more suitable angle.

And so slowly, with one foot in front of the other, grounding my feet into every step I was taking, my inquisitive nature was ready and waiting. I decided to push myself and confront my fears. I said yes to opportunities that scared the shit out of me socially, but I knew they'd help me grow and embrace who I am. I wanted to meet and find those other curious and adventurous types. And this time, there'd be no enclosure or cage. And I'd carry all of my wellbeing tools in my bright yellow rucksack.

It's 2020 as I write this, and many challenges have thrown themselves before me. But I managed to honour myself as promised. I didn't always feel confident, definitely not, but instead of my anxiety holding on and choking me into thinking I can't breathe and move forward, like it was having me believe at the beginning of my story, I've now found some tools and decided to walk with my anxiety, show her kindness, give her patience and hold her hand instead. Kindness, compassion and self-love are my new *sankalpa*, a vow I made to myself to support my ultimate truth.

My first invitation to do something out of my comfort zone was to a women's circle. A few years ago I would've cringed at the thought of entertaining such an invite. Obviously not because I hated the company of women—I'm not just attracted to women, I *love* women. But I've never entirely identified as being completely female. I've always been rather fluid and love gender blending and blurring it up. However, this gave me a chance to be around like-minded women who were all about building a safe place to explore, celebrate body confidence, and raise one another up with love. I went from someone who would nearly choke on my name in a group to the person kicking off the conversations and engaging others by bringing my authentic self to the table. And never once were me or my ideas made to feel like the elephant in the room. Like my yoga teacher, these new soulful friends encouraged me to celebrate my wanderlust for life and the flame within my heart.

My local film house was a gentle way to ease myself out there and meet other queer people that didn't involve feeling over-stimulated by flashing lights or thumping music. I love the Northampton Filmhouse, it's like my second home. It's a small indie art cinema that's cosy and intimate with large, spacious, black leather reclining chairs which provide plenty of leg room so you don't feel like you're sitting on top of one another like sardines packed together. I'd seen that once a month they held a queer film night. The QFilm that I attended alone was the screening of a film called *Cupcakes*, a story about a happy and flamboyant man who signs up his female best friends for an international song contest, similar to the Eurovision, without their knowledge. I always choose to sit in the back row, located only a few steps from the doors. I enjoy the mystery of sitting at the back, where I can watch any film by myself comfortably and quickly disappear afterwards with minimum fuss. These seats are also more accessible which is important to me. I have Ehlers-Danlos syndrome, and when I'm having a flare-up of my painful restless legs, I know I can fidget as much as I need to without distracting the other film-lovers.

The Filmhouse is like the calm in the storm, it's my go-to place to have me-time and indulge my love of cinematography. So I sat on the back row with only one other person to my left in the last chair by the wall. Perhaps because it was the film house and a venue that I was already familiar with, but as I waited for the lights to dim down and *Cupcakes* to begin, I didn't feel any anxiety about the possibility of attending an after-film meet up. I actually felt excited! After the lights came up though, I realized that I didn't know who was here from the QFilm group and those who were simply regular filmgoers out for an evening to watch a cheesy queer film. I decided to wait in the foyer and hoped that I didn't look awkward. Luckily, I didn't have to hover around for too long as I heard a young man mention to one of the ushers that he was a member of the QFilm group but had been running late so he'd missed making an announcement before the beginning of film. He seemed really sweet and easygoing, and so did the other guy he was with. Before I lost my nerve and bottled it, I walked over and introduced myself, explaining that it was my first time at a QFilm evening. They were very welcoming and introduced themselves as Zach and Adam. I took the initiative and invited Zach and Adam to join me for dinner as I hadn't eaten; it would also give us a chance to talk about the film and hangout. I texted KJ the following day to share my excitement. *Hey, I attended the QFilm meet-up last night and it was awesome! I met two lovely guys, who also shared my passion for film and queer arts, and we had a fabulous time putting the world to rights over dinner. I'll call you later to tell you more xx*

A few months later, Zach introduced me to Cat and Liz, who had taken over running the QFilm monthly screenings, and the rest of the group. I'd finally found a queer group I enjoyed *and* felt comfortable in. I loved the diversity and how welcoming everyone was. My new friendships extended outside of the group too, with a couple of us attending gigs, queer theatre, and putting on other events in town together.

When people think of yoga, they see a slim, fit, abled-bodied person making some impressive shapes. Perhaps they're crouching, their legs in the air, between their arms like a frog, or doing a complex balance on their head. But Ali was right when she told me in my first lesson, yoga is much more than those exaggerated poses we see on Instagram. Yoga hasn't just taught me about my own balance and sense of control on the mat. It's also given me the confidence to believe in my own ability off the mat and outside of those big red wooden doors too. I learned that I didn't have to be afraid of opening my heart and feeling vulnerable.

You see, when something painful or unnerving happens to me, I'm transported backwards and reminded of the vulnerable young person I was, frightened of a world that didn't make sense. I was quick to recognise that not all scary monsters hide under the bed, and that compassion and empathy are not everyone's priority or one of their aspirations. So with no coping tools or the required communication skills to articulate this emergent fear, my first reaction for a long time, transitioning from a child, to an adolescent, and then to a young adult, was anxiety. I was vulnerable, a misfit who despite trying very hard to learn and adapt, never quite got it right and carried that frustration and heartache with me everywhere. I'd spent my life always feeling small and never good enough because I was different, surrounded by onlookers who were more than happy to point that out. And my natural response had been to hide away, make myself small and disappear any way I could. I didn't believe I was strong enough or brave enough to go against the grain to be myself, and I carried a heavy rucksack crowded full of shame and the unkind voices of society with me everywhere.

But then I'm reminded on days like today that I'm not a powerless person anymore. I'm not afraid of the world even when it still doesn't make sense. Sure, I still hold the scars and the memories haven't faded, but my experiences have taught me I'm resilient, and they've given me a deeper sense of wisdom and power. If you can't find the compassion around you, and you've witnessed all too well how fear and judgement only fuels the fire within, the natural conclusion is to develop this empathy yourself, *for* yourself and that precious child who lives within. It's like a piece of my mind connects deep into my soul and my inner warrior emerges.

I'm aided with plenty of strength, and I refuse to be defeated. I carry with me decades of unbelievably painful experiences and encounters. Times where fear gripped my every move and more often than not, I was standing on the edge of my sanity. For years, I'd believed myself not strong enough to take another step forward or face another day. I'd felt weak, but deep down I knew, really *knew* that I didn't want to lose. So I kept fighting, even when my hands were raw, I maintained some faith and hope, and held on, that little bit longer, and that little bit tighter. Until one day, much later on, I woke up and realised that the moment had passed and I was no longer hurting and most importantly, I was still alive.

And as these last few years are now proving, as I push myself out of my comfort zone and face demons who have haunted me for far too long, utilizing tools from my yoga lessons such as coherent breathing and ujjayi breathing (to energise and relax) which enable me to ground myself back into any present moment. And by using the half moon or *Ardha Chandrasana* pose to stretch into my power. Here is where I've learnt to recognise and trust in my own ability.

The apprehension of those sinister butterflies who greeted me each morning and swarmed their unease throughout my entire body has lifted. The years of carrying a heavier burden than most because I always felt like such an outsider looking in are still there, but they're a distant memory like a faded photograph. Existing in a society that didn't feel like home, a home kitted out with worn out fraying furniture created by disconnect from everything and everyone around me has now been replaced with the knowledge and satisfaction that I was never a socially awkward misfit. My passion, curiosity, and beautifully queer soul wasn't just accepted when I started to spread my winds in search of an authentic home, they were embraced, invited, and loved by many. And why wouldn't they be? After all, like I thought and hoped, I'm not the only one who has ever felt this way. I'm not unique in viewing life at another angle. There are plenty of us out there excitedly waiting to share our lives with others. And we'd happily stamp on any oppressive cage built to tame and restrict.

My yoga lessons with Ali haven't just given me hope. They've taught me how to see myself again, and how to care deeply for myself and with great love. Each day of my practice something began to grow inside of me, a connection with something deeper than myself.

I'm more than just alive.

I'm actually beginning to live.

The Taxi Driver

by Briony Hastings

Meredith walked to the taxi as quickly as she dared in the unfamiliar heels. She might not know much about nights out, but she was sure that her customary shabby, well-worn boots would look rather out of place. With her little sister away on holiday, the temptation to borrow something a little more glamorous had been too great to resist. She had a moment to regret her choice of sleeveless top though, as the cool night air raised the hairs on her bare arms.

The driver checked her name, and she gave a quick greeting in response. It took a moment of concentrated coordination for her to clamber into the seat, her new jeans sliding a little on the leather.

"Just to the town centre, please," she said and checked her phone as he pulled away from the dark, silent house. Two missed calls and one text from her dad. *Let me know where you're going and what time you'll be back x*

She hesitated. *Changed my mind. Off to bed now xx.* She switched it off and stowed it at the bottom of the too-small clutch bag. The thought of being without her oversized rucksack stabbed anxiety in her chest. She tried not to think of all the things she could have brought—bottle of water, spare pair of shoes, cardigan—though that would certainly raise some eyebrows in a bar. No need to make herself look any more out of place, and maybe it was healthy to cast off the security blanket once in a while, despite her discomfort.

"Night out?" the taxi driver asked. "At least it's stopped raining."

"Yes," she said, watching the way the streetlights shone on the dark, wet pavement. Funny how her own street looked so foreign by night. "I'm just meeting a friend in town." Her face flushed hot with embarrassment. Maybe she'd left at a strange time. Maybe he'd think it odd that she was alone. "I don't do this very often," she said. Maybe it was less awkward, if she highlighted it herself? "Going out, that is. Bit of a new experience. I don't drink, so…"

"Not at all?"

"No, never really got into it." She relaxed a little more into the seat. She was fairly adept at steering a wayward conversation back to safer, more well-charted waters. "And I spent too much time in the library at uni, I guess."

"Oh, my daughter's thinking about her applications now," he said. "Where did you go?"

"Durham. It was good, but yeah… Didn't do much of the socialising, really."

The click of his indicator was loud as they turned onto the main road. "You enjoyed your studies, though?"

She laughed. "Yes and no. It was fine, but I don't…" She wrinkled her nose and watched a raindrop meander haltingly down the window. "I don't love it for its own sake. I do well in the exams, but it's not really what I wanted to do. Sometimes I feel like it was a bit of a waste of time, me going, but…" She shrugged and glanced back in the driver's direction. His eyes met hers in the rear-view mirror.

"Why did you?" he asked.

"Why did I go to uni?" The question surprised her. People didn't ask that. No one bothered interrogating a decision they thought was a correct one. Why check the course of a ship if you were confident in its destination? People made their own assumptions and didn't probe any deeper.

"I…well, it felt more like I would've had to find reasons *not* to go. School wanted me to go, and my parents wanted me to go. I don't know, really. I think poor Dad would have kicked off if I hadn't."

They continued to talk as the car threaded its way unerringly through the late-night traffic. She didn't take many taxis, but the conversation normally petered out after the pleasant small-talk had been politely concluded.

Tonight was different.

They talked about her grades. He groaned at the confession of her low-paid admin job, and she laughed at his implausible suggestions of a more high-powered career away in the city. They talked about his daughter, Sahana, who was studious, and his son, Amrik, who was clever but easily distracted. Meredith told him about her little sister, and how she'd be leaving for university in September after one more summer holiday with the family. He told her about how hard his daughter worked and how proud he was of her.

"Where's your friend meeting you?" he asked as they drew close to the town centre.

"Ah," she said and wavered on the precipice of an unplanned sentence. "I…I lied about the friend." She turned her head back to the window to avoid his gaze. "I wanted to try this. And I didn't have anyone to ask. So it's just me." She gave a little huff of laughter, heavier than she'd intended.

"Oh. Will you be all right?" he asked, his tone sincere. "By yourself?"

"Yeah, I'll be stone-cold sober the whole time," she said. "I'll be fine. Trust me."

"Okay," he said.

She liked the fact that he didn't push the issue. Unlike the worry-turned-interrogation she had grown weary of getting from her parents.

"Where do you want me to drop you?"

She hesitated again. "Up by the Boston?"

"The Boston?" They pulled up at some traffic lights, and the red glow illuminated his face for a moment. "That's… a gay bar, isn't it?"

She closed her eyes and felt that familiar rising dread, a knife twisting in her stomach. She wished, sometimes, that people would just keep their mouths shut. Do her the courtesy of offering the reassurance of plausible deniability. It was always so wounding to hear something hateful from the mouth of someone she'd even momentarily respected. She'd foolishly assumed that the strange anonymity, the lack of history or expectation between the two of them, would make her immune to his disapproval.

"Yes," she said. "I know."

"Oh, just checking," he said, oblivious. "Are you, then?" When she didn't answer, he glanced towards her in the rear-view mirror again. "Gay, I mean."

She checked the road ahead, trying to accurately map their whereabouts. They weren't far away now. If things got awkward, the journey would be over in a minute or so anyway. She'd manage.

"I don't know," she said, her honesty surprising her. Her heart pounded with a painful intensity.

"You don't know?" He chuckled as they turned the corner. "How come?"

"Haven't really thought about it, I guess," she said. No, that wasn't true. "Well. I have thought about it. But I haven't really come to any firm conclusions, so…"

"Okay," he said. "Well, that's all right."

She laughed, swept away by a tidal wave of relief. "If you say so. Sometimes I feel like it isn't." Up ahead of them, the Boston was abuzz with light and movement.

"Your family doesn't know." He indicated to pull up on the side of the road.

It wasn't a question, but she shook her head. "I mean, they might guess. I try not to think about it, to be honest." The passing reference to how her parents *might* react ballooned into an overwhelming, suffocating worry. What if they did know? What if they'd known all this time? What if they laughed about how secretive she tried to be? She shoved the notion back beneath, into the depths where it belonged. "My dad asked where I was going tonight. They're on holiday, and I didn't go with them… He worries. And, I mean, I don't want to feel like he's keeping tabs on me. But I also didn't want to tell him I was coming *here* and have him ask…"

She registered the fact that the journey was over and began to fumble in her bag for the cash.

He switched the engine off. "If you want to talk, we can."

She hesitated.

"I've stopped the meter," he said. "You can pay me for

the journey, it's fourteen quid. But if you want to stay..."

She fished out the money and handed it over. She sat back in her seat, her left hand on the smooth plastic of the door handle, trying to gauge him. His face was still mostly obscured by her angle in the car and by the darkness. He didn't seem creepy. He didn't seem homophobic. And she was only a few feet away from safety if he got weird. He seemed nice. He seemed like he actually wanted to listen. And she really wanted to talk to someone, anyone. She spent so much time feeling as if she were broadcasting a panicked, confused distress signal but no one ever came to help. Here, finally, was a response.

She took her hand off the door. "If you're sure," she said. "Don't you have...?" She gestured vaguely. "Don't you have another trip?"

"Eh, it's nice to take a break," he said.

She was comforted by his pleasant tone. Too often, people pretended that they wanted to listen but they had an ulterior motive, or something else on their mind, or an unknown time limit on their tolerance for the conversation. He didn't sound tense, or distracted, or impatient. "Okay," she said and clicked her seatbelt free.

"So, you like girls?"

She laughed again, caught off-guard by the bluntness of the question. "I..." She made an inarticulate noise of indecision. "I think I might. But it's hard to tell, I guess. I've never really dated people, and it's hard to get into dating people when you don't even know if you're into them or not."

"Well," he said. "Do you like boys?"

She made a similar doubtful noise. "I mean, I have liked boys. One boy. Mostly theoretically."

"Theoretically?" He laughed.

"I went to an all girls' school," she said. "Boys were a pretty theoretical subject."

"Okay, okay," he said. "Girls, then. What girls have you liked?"

"Huh," she said and looked out of the window again.

A few teenagers walked past, their conversation loud yet unintelligible through the glass. The sounds were muted, almost as if she were underwater. They glanced over at the stopped taxi curiously, and she averted her eyes. "I…I don't think I've ever said this out loud. Okay." She drew a deep, measured breath. The taxi smelled pleasantly of some citrus air freshener.

"Take your time," he said.

"I had a friend at uni—have a friend, I guess. We were really close, first year. Best friends close. We'd talk basically all day every day, texting backwards and forwards." She rubbed her nose, not sure whether she was explaining herself properly. The words sounded utterly insufficient now she was finally saying them out loud. "But in our second year, she went to study in Australia for her year abroad. The time difference was really hard. We tried to keep it up, but she had a lot of stuff to do. She made new friends. They went to the Great Barrier Reef – on these amazing adventures she'd tell me about. She sent me the photos, obviously, but it wasn't the same. And I'd missed my friends from school first year, so I *knew* what that was like. This was different." She waved her hands hopelessly. She wasn't telling this story properly. She was used to sketching out a few mental drafts before presenting *anything* to an audience. This was her first attempt, and it was showing. "I can't explain it. I felt like I'd lost a limb. I didn't just miss her every now and again—I missed her *constantly*. I just felt so hollow, waiting for her. It was ridiculous. I felt so jealous, and lonely, and I wanted to hug her so badly, it hurt. And I had these dreams over and over, where I'd wake up and she'd be lying in bed next to me."

Someone outside the bar gave a rowdy cheer. She suddenly snapped back to reality and froze. This was a very bizarre, personal conversation to be having in such a venue. "Yeah," she said. "And then I realised that probably wasn't just normal friendship talking, and I had a panic about it. And then I tried not to think too hard about it, because I had enough on my plate. And I've been not thinking about it ever since."

"Mm," he said. "So why did you come here tonight?"

"I don't know." She picked at the zip on her bag. "I don't know why I'm doing any of this. I guess maybe I hope I'll prove something to myself."

"Like what?" he asked.

She glanced up. His eyes were serious in the mirror, but she found it hard to pick up the emotion behind them in the dark and the quiet. It was unsettling but freeing at the same time. She shrugged. "I guess it's like trying on a new outfit." She glanced down at the heels. Certainly not her usual style. "You like the look of it, the way the style suits someone else. And you can think—you can hope—that it might look good on you. But then when you try, you might realise that it doesn't fit after all. Either way, it's embarrassing to try when everybody's watching. So maybe this will be better. If I can figure it out, and be *sure*… And then…"

"And then what?" he asked.

She stifled a smile. "I suppose you've got me there. I don't know that, either. I mean, I know it sounds stupid. I feel stupid, saying it to you now; that I really think one night out doing karaoke in a gay bar is going to tell me something."

"You never know," he said. "And even if it doesn't tell you anything, even if you just have a nice night, that wouldn't be so bad."

"I guess not." She stared at the door handle again, wondering if she should go.

"That's why you've come out here by yourself while your family are away? You don't want to tell them?" he asked gently.

She shook her head.

"You don't think they'd be accepting?"

She hissed a breath through her teeth. "It's not that. Not exactly. Sometimes I'm not sure. Sometimes Dad makes comments. I think they'd be fine, I think. But it's not worth rocking the boat over when I'm not sure."

He nodded, as if thoughtful. "You don't like rocking the boat. You did your exams, you went to university, and now this."

There was a vague pang of disagreement, even annoyance, in her stomach. "I'm sure they'd beg to differ," she said. "I rock it when it matters."

"This doesn't matter?"

"Well, it matters to me, but…"

"Then it matters."

She shook her head, frustrated. "What's the use in an argument, or even the awkward conversation, when it might all be in my head?"

"Where else would it be?"

"You know what I mean." She stared back down at her bag and at her silent, black-screened phone. "I'm being too harsh. I'm sure they'd be fine about it. I just don't want the drama."

"That's okay," he said. "If *you're* okay with that."

She shrugged. "Guess I have to be." She gave a short laugh. "I guess sometimes I don't think I get the credit I deserve for not rocking the boat. That frustrates me." She glared at the phone accusingly. "It feels like Dad wants me to tell him every time I leave the house, and I know it's just that he's worried, but it feels like I haven't put a toe wrong in twenty-two years, and yet he still doesn't trust me. I don't drink." She began to tick off on her fingers. "I don't smoke, I've never done drugs, I've never called him late from a party, I've never got less than an A. I've never even had a boyfriend. And yet it gets me nowhere. I feel like I'm on probation, except I never got the enjoyment of doing the crime in the first place." She sighed and shook her head. "Sorry. Metaphor got away from me."

"No, I know what you mean," he said. "I'm sure he loves you. But that doesn't mean he always knows what's best for you."

"God, I hope not," she said.

He inclined his head. "Parents don't know everything, trust me. We try our best, but…"

He used both hands to give an expansive gesture, as if defeated. She was glad he hadn't tried that while driving.

"Do you think your dad has the life that you'd want? No? Then don't worry about what he thinks of yours."

She shook her head. "If only it was that easy."

"It gets easier," he said.

She looked up at him again and admonished herself that they hadn't really been having an even conversation. He'd asked all the questions, and she'd done all the talking.

"I'm sorry," she said, zipping up her bag. "I've been going on and on. I should let you go."

"Okay," he said.

"Not going to tell me to be careful?" She was only half-joking. It felt too good to be true, to escape a conversation like this without a lecture.

He laughed. "No. I'll try and keep the parenting to a minimum."

"I appreciate it."

"Have a nice night," he said seriously. "And look after yourself."

"I'll try." She reached for the door handle. "Thank you. I really don't do this. I mean, I don't do the going out, obviously. But not the talking, either. Probably hard to believe, considering I haven't shut up for the last—I don't even know what time it is."

"It's no problem," he said. "You should try it more often. It's not so bad."

"Thanks," she said, trying to inject more feeling into it and not dwell on how inadequate the word was. He nodded once in acknowledgement, and she felt a pang of loss as she realised she'd never even seen his face properly, let alone learned his name. She opened the door and stepped out on to the gritty pavement. "Goodnight!" she called, and he waved a hand as she shut the door behind her.

Outside of the warm, quiet cocoon of the taxi, the outside world seemed a little alien. She suppressed another shiver as she walked carefully towards the bar, keeping her eyes fixed on the pavement so as not to trip. She showed her ID at the door, stepped inside, and was immediately enveloped in a swell of noise and colourful light.

The bar was busy but not too crowded. She sidled her way between a few people, head still down, and tried to find a gap to get a drink. The music was loud but not in the unpleasantly overwhelming, lung-vibrating way she'd experienced at the occasional house party. She found a gap at the bar and leaned forward a little, trying to catch someone's attention. The familiar regret and anxiety gnawed at her, and the knowledge that she didn't belong here settled heavily in her stomach. She must look idiotic: a confused, bookish straight girl trying to get a drink at a gay bar, standing awkwardly in her sister's borrowed heels. She considered heading straight back out the door, but she didn't want to have to explain herself to her taxi driver.

"Hey."

Meredith jumped at the soft voice behind her. She turned to see a girl about her own age. She looked a little taller than Meredith, but she also wore much more impressive heels. Her hair was long and dark, and her eyes sparkled beneath large, round glasses. She was wearing a dark red lipstick, flawlessly applied. The smooth bold line contrasted starkly to the pale skin beside it. Meredith had tried putting on her own lipstick only a few hours ago, but she'd seen five-year-olds have more success colouring within the lines and washed it off in despair.

"Whoops. I didn't mean to startle you."

"Sorry, I was in my own world." Meredith tried not to stare and thought of helpless sailors bewitched by sirens.

"Are you trying to get a drink? You need to shout a bit louder," she said. "I'm Alex." She indicated over her shoulder toward a few booths at the side of the room. Her nose ring caught the light a little as she turned her head. "Come sit with us when you've got one. Us girls need to stick together."

"I'm Meredith," she said, but her voice was drowned out by the roar of singing as the music moved to a chorus.

"Come over," Alex extended her pinky finger.

Meredith linked hers with it, rather baffled. Alex's hand was warm and soft. Meredith looked up at Alex's lipstick again and thought that enchanted sailors were understandably helpless. Alex seemed to fit here in a way that Meredith feared she never would. But maybe she was being invited in. And if she could steal glances at Alex's genuine smile for an hour or so, then perhaps trying to shout over the bar for a drink that she didn't want would be worth it.

"Pinky promise?" Alex smiled.

"Yeah, sure." She nodded, hoping her meaning would be clear even with the raucous backdrop. Alex seemed satisfied and gave a wave as she made her way over to a table and disappeared into a booth.

After a few moments of standing on tiptoe and shouting with increasing volume at the back of a bored-looking bartender, Meredith finally got his attention and ordered a lemonade. She hadn't been allowed fizzy drinks as a child, and even now they still held something of an exciting novelty value. She took the cold glass, slippery with condensation, and yelled her thanks before following Alex's path back to her booth.

There was a small cluster of five girls sitting there. Meredith quailed as a couple glanced up at her. Dramatic eyeliner put her hurriedly-applied mascara to shame, and she considered just continuing to walk past them. Alex spotted her and jumped up.

"Hey! Sit down." She clinked their glasses together. "Cheers. What did you get?"

"Oh, just lemonade." Meredith tried to focus on Alex's face and not to feel swamped by the other strangers around her. The booth smelled of sweet fruity drinks and perfumed body spray. "I don't really drink."

"What, really? Not when you're out or not at all?"

Meredith settled a little, feeling safer in this familiar territory, and began to talk. The noise rose and fell like waves around them and for once, she didn't feel wildly out of her depth. It was just chatting. Chatting to a pretty girl with bright eyes and perfect lipstick. Meredith waited for the paralysing, stomach-plunging panic, but it didn't come. The way that Alex rocked forward when she giggled made her smile. She also had a habit of pushing up her glasses and adjusting her hair in the same motion. The unremarkable gesture made Meredith feel secure somehow, as did the warmth of Alex's arm beside her.

At some point, there was a lull in the music, and Alex glanced over her shoulder to see what was happening. A small gaggle of three teenage boys lurched in their direction, arms wrapped around each other's shoulders.

"We need more people doing karaoke," one of them said, his words slightly slurred. "Come on."

"Will's just broken up with his boyfriend," another whispered, indicating the guy in the middle. "We're looking after him."

Will nodded, hair flopping into his face a little, and started an unintelligible sentence that trailed off before Meredith could pin it down. The first boy, apparently sensing a receptive audience, reached for Meredith's hand and tried to pull her to her feet.

"Oh," Meredith said, half-laughing, too distracted to resist, and turned to Alex. "Well, seems I'm urgently needed elsewhere."

"You like karaoke?" Alex asked and smiled.

Meredith attempted a shrug, which was difficult as Will tugged at her arm. "I don't know. I'd quite like to try. It was sort of on the to-do list for the evening." Along with speaking to a cute girl.

Alex winked at her and gave a little wave from behind the drink she was sipping. "In that case, I'm not rescuing you. Have a nice time."

The dance floor was small, sticky, and not very busy. There were two more boys of a similar age arguing with the employee manning the karaoke setup, though he seemed to be taking it in good humour. One of the three who'd fetched Meredith left to join them, leaving her to prop up Will. His arm was heavy around her bare shoulder. Alex's had been much softer and comforting, rather than stifling. Meredith regretted not pulling off a flirty quip about the to-do list.

"My boyfriend dumped me," Will said, leaning close

into her, his breath hot on her cheek and reeking of alcohol. He stumbled on long, slim legs like a baby giraffe.

"Sorry to hear that," Meredith said and patted him on the back in a way she hoped was supportive. It felt strange to hear him talking so openly about a boyfriend. She must have heard a guy say that before, but she found that she couldn't place a memory of it. He continued in a similar vein, telling her about the offending boyfriend. It was a little hard to hear everything he was saying, but she caught enough to agree that he sounded like an absolute wanker.

"What are you doing, Will?" One of the arguing boys had returned and took Meredith's place under Will's arm. "We're supposed to be singing, not moping!" He patted Will's face. "You've got this, okay? You deserve better."

Will nodded so enthusiastically that Meredith feared he'd fall over.

"The guy won't change the line-up," the new boy continued. "He says he's got a few requests to go through first, but he says they're bangers, all right?" He turned to Meredith. "You joining?"

She nodded. At some point the music restarted with a passion, they roped Meredith into a dance formation that most closely resembled the Can-Can, and Will got hold of a microphone that everyone else shouted into.

"Why aren't you singing?" one of the boys bellowed at her, midway through a song that a small screen had announced was *The Ballroom Blitz*.

"I don't know the words," Meredith yelled back.

He rolled his eyes in exasperation. "None of us do. Don't worry, just make it up. Have some fun!"

Meredith wasn't quite sure where the requests list for the karaoke operator had come from, but apparently there were some die-hard fans of this song somewhere in the bar. By the time it played for the third time, she was confident enough to holler the chorus along with the rest of them, something which seemed to cheer even Will up. The six of them careened like a single many-legged creature across the dance floor, and Meredith gave a sheepish wave to Alex as they went.

After that, *We Are the Champions* and *Don't Stop Me Now* came on, both of which Meredith knew well enough to sing along to. When an intense dance track came on, she excused herself to the toilet. When she returned, the DJ played *Mr Brightside*, and she shouted the words until she was hoarse.

At around two o'clock, the bar closed. Meredith drifted out in a daze, waved her good-byes, and assured the six not-so-strangers that she'd be fine on her own. She headed to McDonald's and ordered a milkshake.

She walked back down the street a little and sat on a low wall by the bus station to take the weight off her feet. She didn't regret wearing the heels, though. They certainly weren't for everyday use, but they made her feel dainty and attractive, which was a novel experience. What had Alex thought of them?

She was still hot from the dancing. Her milkshake was too frozen to drink, so she stirred it idly and enjoyed a moment of quiet. The wall was cold and probably dirty, but she could throw her jeans in the wash tomorrow without anyone to comment. Her eyes felt a little dry from the contact lenses. She always felt unattractive in her glasses, but Alex looked damned good in hers. Meredith was also sure that her hair had long since escaped her attempt at styling it, but she couldn't bring herself to care.

She'd expected to feel something more in this moment, but she found herself oddly comfortable with the lack of any epiphany. She felt peaceful and unmoored, floating in a dark silent sea alone. She glanced up at the sky above. The stars were mostly obscured by the light pollution and the passing clouds, but a few bright ones still shone there. She smiled at them. It crossed her mind that anyone watching her would probably think she was drunk. There was something oddly reassuring about that, some strange sanctuary from judgement. Her mind felt quieter than it had done in a long time. A ridiculous cliché of serenity, but a welcome one. She felt the breeze ruffle her hair, like cool fingers brushing past her face.

She stayed staring up at the stars as she slowly drank her melting milkshake. She was in no rush to leave. She wondered where her taxi driver was, and whether she'd ever see him again. He was probably busy providing some sage advice to a car full of boisterous teenagers. The thought made her smile.

She imagined telling him about her evening. He'd smile at the confession that she'd almost left the bar immediately but didn't want to disappoint him. He'd nod when she told him about daring to sit with Alex. And he'd laugh when she'd say that she'd still had the chance to do some dancing. It was nice, somehow, to feel like she'd shared this evening with someone. She felt proud of herself tonight, and she thought he would be too.

Milkshake finished, she gave a long peaceful exhale and pulled out her phone to call for a taxi. Maybe she'd get to share her story with him after all.

Red Lipstick
by *Claire Deacon*

The lipstick was for courage. I wasn't usually the type of person to be nervous about attending a group where I didn't know anyone. In the past I'd shown up alone to writing groups, burlesque classes, music festivals, and a samba band workshop with no worries at all. But tonight was different. There was so much more at stake, and the red lipstick helped. I needed it to project a confidence I was lacking.

I'd found the bi women's group online, and they were based in London. I'd booked in at a Travelodge on the South Bank so I didn't have to worry about leaving early to catch the train home. As I put on my makeup in the hotel room, I wondered what the other women there would be like. Would they be friendly? They seemed to be from our brief conversations online, but you could never quite tell until you met someone in person. What if they were already a tight-knit clique, with their own in-jokes and expectations? Would I seem hopelessly provincial next to their London lifestyles? There was only one way to find out. I took a deep breath, pulled on my cutest heels, and walked out into the evening.

It was spring, but only just, and the chill in the air hastened my steps. My singular focus on the night ahead meant I didn't take in my surroundings the way I normally would. On any other night I'd revel in all the things I love about London. The tall, imposing buildings, the sense of endless possibilities, and the sheer number of people make me feel anonymous. London turns me into an observer. I can walk by, just another face in the crowd, and notice the loved-up couples, the stressed-out employees, and of course, the cute women. No one knows who I am and no one asks for my story. But tonight, by going to the group, I was deliberately leaving my anonymous comfort zone. Adrenaline rushed through my veins with every step I took.

The high heels were a bad idea. Geography has never been my strong point, and I'd completely misjudged the distance to the venue. By the time I found Topolski, a trendy-looking bar nestled under the Waterloo railway arches, my feet were throbbing and my heart was hammering. Maybe I should just go back to the hotel, order a pizza, and forget this whole bisexual business. No. I wasn't getting blisters for nothing, damn it. And I hadn't come all the way to London just to sit in a Travelodge watching Love Island and eating lukewarm pizza. I pushed open the door to the bar.

It was warm and crowded, people pressing in on me from all sides, and the dramatic change in temperature from the chilly air outside made my head swim. A woman gave me a dirty look as I accidentally bumped into her, and I hoped that she wasn't part of the group. I messaged Cass, the group organiser, to say I was there.

We're at a table round the corner, near the bar.

I rounded the corner and there they were. Were it not for the small Pride flag on the table, I would never have guessed that this group of women were bisexual. There was no unifying look or type; some wore comfy T-shirts and some wore pretty dresses, some were clearly the life of the party and others seemed quieter. I was relieved to see that this was somewhere I could be myself, without having to prove my queerness. Before coming here tonight I'd second-guessed my outfit and makeup multiple times, wondering if there was some sort of bi dress code I should be wearing to fit in and be taken seriously. With my long hair, high heels, and penchant for red lipstick, I don't fit the average person's image of a queer woman. But the whole point of coming here was to be my true self, and that included the part of me that enjoys putting on my femme armour for a night out.

I recognised Cass from her online profile. She spotted me, waved, and gave me a friendly smile. I relaxed just a bit, ordered a drink from the bar, and went to join them.

"Hi," she said, giving me a hug. "It's good to meet you, Claire. This is Erika."

She introduced me to the blonde woman she'd been talking to. Erika leaned across and kissed me on both cheeks like we were old friends.

"I can't believe you've come all the way from Northampton. I'm so impressed."

"It's not as far away as Londoners tend to think, but we don't have any bi-specific groups there and I thought it was about time I joined one."

They clinked their glasses to mine and welcomed me into their conversation. They told me about their jobs, hobbies, and children. Erika told me about the ex-girlfriend who'd recently broken her heart, and Cass told me about her girlfriend, whom she'd met through the group. Both of them were out to most of the important people in their lives, which I really admired them for. After a lifetime of hiding from everyone, including myself, I wasn't sure I'd ever be able to match up to their level of bravery. Then again, I'd found the courage to come here tonight, so maybe I was selling myself short.

"So, Claire, what's your story?"

There it was—the big question, the one I'd spent so many years avoiding. But hadn't I come here tonight to finally share my story? Though it was scary, it was time to start opening up.

I started at the beginning, explaining how I'd barely heard the word bisexual when I was growing up, and when I did, it was never in a positive light. It had seemed like bisexuals, if they really existed, were indecisive, promiscuous, and guaranteed to break your heart. Certainly not someone that you would want to get into a serious relationship with. So although I knew that I liked girls as well as boys when I was a teenager (I didn't know of any other genders back then), I told myself I couldn't be bisexual because I didn't fit those stereotypes. I figured I must really be straight or gay, and my sexuality would come down on one side or the other eventually.

But it didn't happen. So instead I made a deal with myself. Because I liked boys too, I could just focus on them, ignore my same-sex feelings, and everything would be okay. At the time, the prospect of actually telling anyone about any of this was out of the question. Homophobic bullying was rampant at my school, and I assumed that the rest of society would be the same. This avoidance strategy became easier to follow when I got into my first relationship with a man. It was an all-consuming, deeply unhealthy one and for the first few years of it, I didn't have eyes for anyone else or the mental space to think about my sexuality. But after six years, when I'd realised how toxic he was and had made a plan to leave, I began to notice women again. A long-dormant part of me had come back online, reminding me that there was so much more to life than the constricting relationship I was in. Maybe once I was free of him I could finally explore my same-sex desires. It was an exciting thought.

After I'd left him and settled into a flat of my own, I joined a dating site, hoping to meet women. Society seemed to be slightly more accepting of bisexuality by this point, I was out to a few friends, and I was ready and eager for the world of same-sex dating. That world, however, was not ready for me. Most of the local "women seeking women" were quite clear on their profiles that they weren't interested in dating bi women. More than once I was faced with statements like, "I don't want to be anyone's experiment." I could understand not wanting to be messed around or seen as a same-sex experiment, but did the fact that I'd dated one man really mean that no woman would want to date me? From this small pool of profiles, it seemed so. Although I now know that not every gay woman thinks this way, back then it was enough of a blow to extinguish my fragile confidence and convince me that it was hopeless. I headed back into my self-imposed closet.

Six years later I was settled in a great relationship with a wonderful man. He knew I was bi but it wasn't something we talked about, and I was acutely aware that to the outside world I appeared to be straight. This disconnect between my outer and inner identities bubbled away in the background but I managed to push it down and life was fairly uneventful, until 2013 when my world was shattered by the loss of my dad.

It was a terrible year in which I struggled through grief and debilitating health problems. At times I was sure I'd never be happy or healthy again. But, eventually, the clouds began to lift. And when they did, I knew that I couldn't carry on living the way I had before, appearing to the world to be one thing but knowing that I was actually something else. Although it had seemed harmless ignoring my "gay side" all these years, I finally realised what a huge toll it had taken on my mental health, adding an extra layer of stress to everything I did. After losing my dad, I truly understood the painful lesson that life is short, and you never know how long you're going to be here. It was time I started living more truthfully while I still had the chance, and a good first step seemed to be to find my tribe and make some bi friends. That's where the group came in.

"Wow, you've been through a lot," said Erika, giving me a hug once I'd finished my story. "Well done for coming tonight."

I wasn't used to talking about myself so much or so honestly, but it was a relief to finally tell all of this to people who would understand. For years, I'd been splitting myself in two. Depending on where I was trying to fit in, I'd always felt too straight or too gay, so there was always part of me I was trying to supress. Here, with these women, I could be my whole self. I let out a breath, one I'd been holding for a long time.

I relaxed back into further conversation, relieved the focus was no longer solely on me. It was so easy to talk to Erika and Cass. They were slightly older than me and had different life experiences to me, but we clicked straight away.

I could easily have talked to them all night but decided I should introduce myself to some of the other members of the group too. I got chatting to Hayley and Priya, and we bonded over our shared love of music. Priya was a singer and Hayley organised music festivals, and we all agreed that we should go to a gig together soon.

When, sometime later, Hayley said she should start making her way home, I looked at my phone and was stunned to see several hours had gone by. The group was winding down, and I was one of the last ones left. I didn't want to leave yet. It was like I'd just found where I belonged after a whole lifetime of searching, and I was reluctant to give it up. Logically, I knew that there'd be plenty more opportunities to meet up with the group, but it was still hard to tear myself away from them. I hugged each of my new friends and promised I'd see them at the next meetup, a burlesque night in Camden.

My walk back to the hotel was very different from my walk earlier in the night. I had a big smile on my face and my body was alive with happiness rather than nerves. The evening had surpassed my tentative hopes and introduced me to women who would become wonderful friends. In the years that followed, I danced with them in gay bars, cried with them over break-ups, and cheered with them at London pride, dressed in our best pink, purple, and blue coloured finery.

When I got back to my hotel room, I looked in the mirror and realised my red lipstick had completely worn off. I smiled at my reflection. I'd been too busy chatting and making friends to even think about reapplying it. But it had done its job and given me the confidence I needed to get out there. The rest? That was up to me.

Boxed In and Coming Out
by Phoebe Gracey

All I want is to find my box and for people to know that's my box. I have no idea what it will look like or how I'll know it's mine. Will it have my name, Phoebe, written in big letters on the front? Will it come in my favourite colour, have a rainbow pattern, or simply be an old and tatty, plain brown box? Is this box going to fall on top of my head, or will it simply be lurking on a shelf waiting for me to spot it? I just don't know. What I do know is that I'm frantically looking for where my box is, I'm trying to discover where I fit in as a person in this world, and I'd like to know how everyone knows what my box is. I wonder if my box will make a difference, or if I even actually need it. Do I want this box for me or for the rest of society?

At secondary school, everyone had figured people out. Remember when you were fourteen, picking out your GCSEs, and had the whole world sussed? You knew what everyone was like, who to trust, who would be a good friend forever, and who was going to succeed. (Well, guess what? You were probably wrong. The people you thought you knew, changed. The people you thought you could trust stabbed you in the back, and your good friends disappeared as soon as you left school. And the people you thought wouldn't succeed? They are doing amazingly!)

I was always told, "You're one of us, one of the lads." That confused me. I'm not a lad—I'm very much a lass. But, you see, I don't *fit* in with all the girls because I don't wear makeup, I tie my hair back, and I certainly didn't wear a skirt to school. I was wearing wide-leg trousers, a load of bracelets, and my sleeves are rolled up. Conversations of how fit Robert Pattinson was in Twilight didn't appeal to me at all. Much to my delight, people never questioned me or my sexuality. I had a boyfriend so of course there were no questions. I was conforming, and in their eyes, I was straight. Why I was called a tomboy because I didn't conform to society's idea of what it means to be a girl, I'm still yet to understand! I was a girl at school, and I'm a girl now. I have no desire to be a boy or man, so tomboy didn't fit me. I didn't want that label because this wasn't me nor was it how I saw myself. The search went on.

I'm very lucky. For the most part, my generation are very open, but there are some things that we still believed when we were younger. For example if you were bisexual then you were greedy. If you were a girl and said another girl was pretty that was a sure sign she was a lesbian. My eraser told me everything I needed to know about my future from simply flipping and seeing if it landed on the yes or no side. It will just take until the day I die for *everyone* to know I'm gay.

I find it so much easier to get on with guys than girls, and I always have. I guess I just knew where I stand with them. At school, I didn't want to snog their face off and we often had the same interests; a girl doing a double engineering GCSE to society seemed to scream something! Not to my generation but to the older generation. So many times I was told that I was putting myself in a male-dominated world and I'm not part of that because I was a girl. But I'll give as good as anyone else gives when it comes to banter, which often throws the guys…something I take great pleasure in. Getting on with girls is far more complex. I find it hard to know where I stand with them, and that can sometime be made worse when your friend is straight and you're gay, or your gay friend fancies you, but they're so not your type… Why do some of the best ones have to be straight?!

Anyway, back to coming out. It doesn't simply happen once. It's not a case of "just so you know, I'm gay" and then you're done with it. No. You have to keep saying it over and over and over! To everyone you meet. Well, not *everyone*.

I mean, I don't go around Costa telling all the baristas I'm a lesbian, but you get my meaning... And it's not that I'm sick of everyone presuming I'm straight or anything, but it is getting a little annoying. I'm even thinking about having a rainbow tattoo where everyone and anyone can see it, but people could mistake it for me really, really supporting the NHS during the COVID-19 pandemic. Why do I need to tell everyone that I'm gay? Why can't the world get its head around the fact that not everyone is straight?

So, my friends, let's start with the easy part of my coming out story. My friends all absolutely support me. I knew that they would so I didn't have any concerns about coming out to them. I made sure to choose my moment still. It wasn't like we became friends and straight away I told them I was gay, but it always came out quite naturally. I'm really close to my best friend, Jess, and we spend a lot of time at her house; lots of cold evenings sat on the sofa with a film on and blankets wrapped around us to keep warm and cosy even though the heating is on. Movies always lead to lots of conversations about all sorts of things, and there's something about late nights with your best friend that makes you open up to a whole new level. One night, Jess had questions about my disability (like how being a wheelchair user can affect how a relationship works) and that was the point that I chose to tell her I was gay. Two young women talking about sex isn't uncommon these days, and we were both single, which definitely played a part in the conversation. I'd recently broken up with my boyfriend and Jess asked if I'd be getting into another relationship soon. It was something I'd been thinking about, but I knew that my next relationship would be with a woman.

Jess and I worked together, and when my relationship ended, the manager asked if me and Jess were a couple because we spent so much time together. We *had* been spending more time together, but that was simply because we *had* more time *to* spend together now that I was single! Anyway, I told Jess that our manager thought we were together and that her theory wasn't entirely wrong because I am into women.

I expected silence. Or at least a pause. But no. Jess instantly asked how long I'd felt that way. I explained that I'd been thinking about my sexuality for a while, and that the last relationship was the tipping point. That's when I realised that I wasn't being true to myself. I didn't like boys in *that* way. Sure, they were great for conversation and a laugh. But I didn't want to do anything else with them. Previously I thought of myself as bisexual, but another relationship with a man is not something I see in my future. That was the end of me coming out to Jess. It certainly led onto some interesting conversations about our past experiences, and it made us closer. Jess supports me no matter what, as long as I'm happy and being treated right.

All of my friends were absolutely rocked when I came out to them. They like me for *me*: my personality, humour, charm and my determination to succeed in life. They say that as long as my choices make me happy and I'm not breaking the law, it doesn't matter to them. It's my life. And that's a big thing. It is my life, but it isn't my choice. I'm happy with who I am, and it's great that I have friends around me who are cool with me being gay. Ultimately though, if one of my friends *was* unhappy about it, they'd meet my middle finger pointed rigid and could disappear out of my life.

My family.

It's been much harder to come out to them. I soon learned that I have to be more reserved with them. The coming out conversation happened over the phone so I could easily end the call if I needed to. For the most part, my family just want me to be happy. But that's tinted with a mark, like when you accidentally put a white shirt through the washing machine with a red sock and the white shirt is now a shade of pink. It's not ruined, but it's not quite perfect anymore.

"You can be with anyone as long as they make you happy...except for the certain few."

I'm very much aware of who she means when she says, "the certain few," (and that would be another story entirely!) and those people do make me happy, but luckily for Mum, not in a relationship way! It doesn't stop me wondering what would happen if we were in a relationship. Would I still be a member of the family if I did end up in a relationship with someone they didn't like? Would they welcome that person with open arms? Or would they make that person very aware of how much they disapprove of the relationship? I want to know why it's not okay for me to be in a relationship with those people, but would their answer reveal that they aren't actually supportive of the LGBTQ+ community? And if that's the case, do they really even support me? Are they concerned that if I'm in a relationship with "one of those people," I won't give them grandkids? Is it because they know that some people know exactly what my family can be like? They still slip up from time to time when it comes to discussing my preferences, but I simply let it blow over and pretend it didn't happen. Yes, I'm worried about the answers. People say, "Don't ask the question if you don't want the answer," so I haven't asked. And I may never ask.

Whilst my experience with coming out to my family hasn't been a smooth one, and I have a feeling it will never be a smooth ride with them, I don't let their opinions get in the way of what I want for me. There was a reason I came out to my friends first. I half expected things to go wrong with coming out to my family, and I wanted to be able to depend on my friends. That was very much what happened, and my friends reminded me that it doesn't matter what my family think. I have to think of myself first. *I* have to make sure I'm happy. I've been told that sometimes the best family are the people we choose to be our family, and those people will always be there for me.

You'd think that coming out to my family and friends would mean the end of my coming out story. That I'd found the box I was desperately searching for. I suppose in some way you could say that I've found my box. But after a lot of soul searching, it turns out the box wasn't a real thing and that it doesn't make a difference to this story. I've found where I fit in and I don't need a box.

But even if I had found a literal box and even if I carried

it around with me all day, every day, I'd still have to keep coming out! The box doesn't help the situation. People still wouldn't automatically know I was gay, and I'd still have to keep coming out to all the new people I meet.

We live on a big planet with billions of people. We never stop meeting people. I met this one guy, let's call him Frank, through a mutual interest, and we got to chatting outside of our interest. He's a lovely guy, and I get on really well with him. We could talk for hours and were often up until one a.m. sending each other messages. In hindsight, I should have told him sooner, should've done all the *coming out* all over again. So one evening, I'm just chilling on my bed in my PJs with the lights off, and I should be asleep. But instead, me and Frank have been messaging for a while when *that* question came up. The big question. "Are you in a relationship?" When you get that question from straight guys and you're a lesbian, it can be a bit awkward. I said I wasn't, but what I didn't say was that I was into girls. Why didn't I say it? Why didn't I put him out of his misery when it was obvious what was happening? Because it was too personal, and I felt like I'd be exposing myself way too soon. We'd often chatted about how we felt we could be so open and honest with each other, but it didn't feel right, and it seemed too soon to say. What did I get back from Frank? A big smiley face and "I'm single too!"

Now I didn't have a choice—again. I *had* to tell him that I was gay so he didn't think there was a chance of him getting into a relationship with me. I thought I'd make a bit of a joke about it and explained there was a flaw to me being single: so many lovely guys, but I didn't swing that way and all the women I knew didn't swing my way. The delay before his next message seemed to drag on. Was that the end of our friendship? But eventually, my phone pinged. I hesitated, hoping that the reply would be a positive one. I'm glad to say that it was. Frank said it was the most subtle way someone had ever told him they were gay, and the best way of being told someone wasn't into him. I didn't know what to say, but I felt the need to apologise. Strange that, don't you think? That I thought I should apologise for being me, for something I don't have a choice in or control over? People say sorry all the time, and so they should. But should I apologise for who and what I am?

Frank seemed completely okay with me being gay. Coming out to someone is always a concern. Will they be upset? Is our friendship over? But he was cool with it, and our friendship continues to this day. We still stay up chatting till ridiculous o'clock in the morning, but now I'm his wing woman, we chat about girls all the time, and are still just as open and honest.

The journey of self-discovery is a battle but it's enlightening and so very worth it. The coming out experience for me has been ninety percent fantastic and most people have supported me, but it's not the end of my journey. The journey will carry on for the rest of my life, and I'm really excited about what that might bring.

I've found my box but I'm not *defined* by my box.

If you're looking for your box, try to understand that it won't necessarily have all the answers when you find it. Know that it doesn't mean your journey has finished. You get to continue your journey for the rest of your life.

And know that it's an exciting one, so try to enjoy it the best you can.

Make sure to have a laugh.

Live each day for the day that is it.

Remember the next day is a new day.

Get rid of the people that are toxic in your life.

And be the person you wish was there for you when you were young.

Dance of the Bees

by A.J. Herbert

As the final seconds of *Chandelier* echoed out to the hall, Noah completed the last of his many pirouettes. They weren't as masterful as you might see on the professional stage, but he enjoyed every last one as much as he had enjoyed choreographing the piece with Mrs Rhoda.

He walked to his designated spot on the floor, dipped his head, and focused on the mark he had etched into the wood the day before.

He'd always wanted to be a star.

As the only boy in his school's dance troupe, he would always stand out. Sure, he lived in a small village in the middle of nowhere. But once he was older, he'd head to the bright lights of the big city, the city that would make his dreams come true.

There was a momentary pause when the music stopped. It was the calm before the storm. The first claps and cheers began to shower over the troupe, prompting all five of them to lift their heads and revel in the applause.

The hundred or so other children and staff members respond in unison. *This is only the beginning.*

He'd barely grinned when a new sound began to emerge. It bulldozed its way through to his ears at a lower pitch than the cheers coming from the rest of the hall.

The new and unfamiliar sound grew louder before a couple of the teachers at the back of the hall moved in to do what teachers do.

Mrs Rhoda stomped onto the stage and ushered them to the side. Noah watched as Mrs Rhoda made herself taller than normal; she was like a giant towering over the children sat in front of the stage.

"Well, well, well, children. That was truly magnificent!"

Her voice boomed across the hall. Everyone in the room looked her way. No one dared to whisper in her presence.

"Thank you to our wonderful and talented Year 4 dance group. This was their first performance and will not be their last." She glanced at Noah and smiled. "They'll be performing at our open day in a couple of weeks and will once again demonstrate how magnificent and inventive our pupils are. I hope you'll all join us. Now, please exit the hall one year group at a time."

Noah was full of pride. He had delivered on his promise to put on a performance, and Mrs Rhoda had responded by showering him and his dance troupe with praise.

As the classes began to leave, Mrs Rhoda turned to face Noah and his friends.

"Excellent job, all. If you could just exit to the back of the stage for now, I'll be with you in a minute."

As the five of them began to move, Noah held back to see what Mrs Rhoda was going to do next.

"Mr Crawford, can you find out who wanted to show their 'appreciation' in that manner?"

"Of course I can. No problem."

Noah was intrigued. He smiled. Mrs Rhoda wanted to brag about how wonderful her dance troupe was…and they were. Rather than join the rest of his troupe, who were rushing down the steps into the back-stage area, he decided to listen in on the conversation. No doubt she'd tell Mr Crawford all about how fabulous Noah was and how she was certain he'd be a star one day.

"Seriously, what the hell was that?" Mrs Rhoda asked.

Mr Crawford's response was mumbled.

Noah thought he heard the words "object" and "joining in," but he couldn't figure out why they were being used.

"Get me names, please. I want names."

Aware that he might be caught listening, Noah turned and ran to join the girls.

"Great performance, all of you. You really put a smile on

people's faces." She looked at each of them before her gaze rested on Noah. "Are you okay, Noah?"

Noah glanced back toward the stage and took a deep breath. *Don't let it show.* He looked up and grinned. "I couldn't be happier."

***

Alex sat in the staff room at lunch time, picking at the loose skin around his nails. Anything to distract him from thinking about what he'd witnessed during the assembly. Noah's difference wasn't even accepted at this early age.

Alex had been at the school for six weeks now, on the second and final teaching practice of his PGCE. His positive assessment scores meant his dreams of becoming a good teacher were coming to fruition. And yet his decision to pursue a teaching career had always been accompanied with an internal worry. Not all would welcome a gay teacher.

In his darkest moments, he pondered the words of anonymous online users who took delight in professing their homophobic views. In their eyes the question was clear: how could children be taught by someone who is inherently "immoral?" Those people were dangerous and no better than the perverts and cold-blooded murderers given life sentences for their sins.

Whilst others on his teaching course had known of his sexuality from day one, he'd taken great care to ensure that none of the university staff or teachers from either of his teaching practices had learned of his secret. Alex had deliberately and successfully censored his behaviour to ensure he fell under the radar.

"I thought it was a marvellous performance," said Miss Taylor. "It reminded me of the video but was different enough to be its own thing. And they are only eight. I wish I could have danced like that at that age… I wish I could dance like that now!"

"It was definitely a performance all right." Mrs Standford chimed in. "That boy is going to get loads of attention from the girls, isn't he? Adorable little thing. What's his name? Nathan, Nick?"

"Noah," said Mr Andrews. "But I don't think he'll ever reciprocate that attention."

Alex's heart raced. He knew what Mr Andrews was getting at. He'd always made it clear that "boys should be boys."

"What do you mean?" replied Mrs Standford. She stirred her tea a little more vigorously.

Mr Andrews rolled his eyes and made a limp-wrist gesture. "The kid is a total fag."

Alex clenched his jaw, as if that could protect him from the stabbing effect of Andrews' words. He'd known life as a gay teacher wouldn't be easy, but he thought that his colleagues would be on his side. They weren't supposed to be the enemy. *Stay calm.*

Miss Taylor shook her head. "You can't say that. He's only eight. No child knows what they are at eight."

"Well, he's certainly making it obvious, prancing around like that. If he wants to make things easy for himself, he should just act like all the other boys. None of this dance business."

"Oh, well, I didn't think about that," whispered Mrs Stanford.

"You shouldn't need to, Helen," said Miss Taylor. "It's 2020. Children can be whoever they want to be." She glared at Mr Andrews. "He could end up being the biggest ladies' man on the planet when he's older, but right now, as an eight-year-old child, he's found a way to express himself that makes him happy. Maybe you should do the same."

Mr Andrews huffed. "It's not worth trying to reason with a twenty-first century snowflake," he said quietly. "What do you think, mate?"

As the only other male teacher in the room, Alex assumed the question was for him. He took a quick scan of the room and avoided prolonged eye contact with Mr Andrews.

"I…I'm not sure what I think of the situation." He focused on his trousers and flicked away some imaginary fluff, hoping that would be an end to this uncomfortable conversation. Mr Andrews was goading him, trying to get a reaction from someone that was not like him, the socially-pushed embodiment of red-blooded masculinity.

"Come on, Alex. You must have an opinion. No one likes a fence-sitter."

"Leave him alone, Michael," Miss Taylor said. "Go and get started on your Sports Day plans already, you're already behind."

Miss Taylor smiled in Alex's direction, and he appreciated the abrupt end to the unwelcome conversation.

For the next school week, Alex had been asked to teach the Year 4 class. Their regular teacher had shared her lesson plans with him, and Alex had spent the weekend memorising them.

He was eager to do well, but he walked into the classroom on Monday morning with butterflies in his stomach.

He was going to be teaching a class that included a child that Mr Andrews had labelled a "fag." Alex's deep fear that people might notice similar characteristics in him could lead them to connect the dots.

Where Noah's stereotypical traits could be dismissed with the innocence of childhood, that wasn't the case for Alex. A negative response from concerned parents could call his promising career to a premature end.

As the week progressed, Alex found ways to ensure he focused more on the tasks at hand. Teaching a younger age group allowed him to explore his teaching personality further. Story time was a favourite part of his day, where he could vividly inhabit the book's characters, and bring age-old tales to life with his own unique interpretation. His ability to effortlessly switch from pantomime villain to gallant hero, through the use of revealing accents and expressive movement had gone down well with the class.

By Thursday's maths class, he'd settled in. Whilst this was his first experience of teaching a younger class, he'd taken to it like a duck to water. *This was definitely the right career for me.*

Alex had received praise for the way in which he had adapted to his new surroundings, particularly from Miss Taylor, the teacher who had come to his rescue in the staffroom.

The thought of a premature outing was still stuck in the back of Alex's mind, particularly if Mr Andrews continued to probe him in the same manner, but for now Alex took comfort in his ability to just teach. He split the class into groups of five and tasked them with an exercise on calculating square numbers.

He moved from table to table to check on the progression of each group. When he got to Noah's table of five, three boys and two girls, Alex noticed that Noah and the girls sat together, but the other two boys were much further away.

"Boys, is there any reason you're not working with the rest of your group?"

Charlie looked up and gave Alex an anxious look. "My mummy said that I can't sit next to Noah." He paused, clearly not sure why. "She doesn't want me to 'catch' what he has."

Alex's palms began to sweat as he grappled with his inability to form an immediate response. None of his teacher training had prepared him for this. Asking Charlie what he meant would only draw attention to their conversation, and he clearly didn't understand anyway. Noah seemed completely oblivious, but Alex was sure he'd looked for a re-assurance when Charlie spoke.

"I can promise you both that you won't *catch* anything from any child in this classroom." In the most charming tone he could muster, he proclaimed, "I have it on good authority that everyone in this room has a clean bill of health!"

Alex waited for an accepting response from the self-isolated outcasts. The anticipation was almost too much to bear.

"Oh, okay," said Charlie.. "I guess we can move over to the rest of our group."

The two boys picked up their chairs and joined the remainder of the group. Alex felt a wave of relief, but a leaden weight settled in his stomach, knowing that the crisis had only been averted for now. Remembering back to his own school days, this treatment of Noah wouldn't end any time soon. Something had to be done.

***

As the clock struck half three on Friday, Noah found himself alone in the corner of the room, staring intently at the beige carpet. All the other children in his class had been collected by their parents.

"Everything all right, Noah?" asked Mr Moses.

He didn't respond. He wanted nothing more than to be at home, spending his weekend reading the next book in his Roald Dahl collection.

"You did well this week. You're as good at maths as I am," Mr Moses said.

Noah glanced in the direction of his teacher. "You think so?"

"Yes, I do. You're a real maths genius."

Noah showed his appreciation with a small smile, though he felt anything but happy.

"Is everything okay?"

Noah didn't really know how to respond. He'd thought that his performance last week would gain him more friends, but that hadn't happened. He'd tried to ignore the whispering and giggling from the other children. They were talking about him but not to him, but he had no idea why.

"Sir, do you think I'm a bad person?"

"Absolutely not. Why do you ask that?"

"Well, Vashti told me today that some of the children think I'm unwell. They say that I'm contagious, and because I'm not like the other boys, there's something wrong with me."

"You look perfectly healthy to me, Noah. Do you feel unwell?"

Noah thought about the question. It seemed rather silly. "No, Sir. I feel fine."

"That's good, then. Noah, you're a bright and talented

young boy. I saw how marvellously you and your friends performed in assembly. Always be proud of who you are. Be who you want to be."

Noah chuckled to himself. "I like bees. They keep us all alive, did you know that?"

"I most certainly did. The keepers of the earth."

Noah began to feel happier. His teacher had made it clear to him that he was a good person. Nobody was going to make him feel otherwise. Maybe he would learn a new dance routine this weekend, something he could share with his dance troupe on Monday. The only way was forwards.

It was perfect timing as his parents approached the classroom door.

***

The following Monday's assembly followed the same, well-trodden journey as the hundreds that had preceded it. Announcements were read, a story was told and the assembly ended with a presentation. This week it was time to congratulate the pupils who had full attendance for the previous term. "Now, you'll remember that a couple of weeks ago, some of the Year 4 children put on a dazzling dance performance for you all."

A round of applause echoed through the assembly hall.

Noah exchanged smiles with the girls in his dance troupe. The school had remembered their performance, and it felt fantastic.

"Whilst most of you showed your appreciation for the performance, unfortunately some did not do."

Noah noticed that a few people had turned to look in his direction. He wasn't sure why but assumed it had something to do with what Mrs Rhoda had just said. Who hadn't shown him the same appreciation? Was this why people had called him "unwell?"

Grace, one of the girls in his dance troupe put her arms out to give him an air hug, something they'd done ever since they started dancing together as a way of comforting each other when something was difficult or too hard to learn.

Noah replied to Grace with an air hug of his own. Some of the Year 6 boys began walking towards Mrs Rhoda, until they were all lined up and facing the rest of the school.

Noah recognised them all; they were the boys that took over the playground at lunch times and told everyone where they could play and what they could do.

But he was surprised to see that all of them looked ashamed, and they seemed to be trying to avoid eye contact with the hall.

"These boys have something they would like to say to the Year 4 group," said Mrs Rhoda.

"We're sorry," they said in unison.

"And what are you sorry for?" asked Mrs Rhoda.

One of the boys stood forward. "We're sorry that we didn't appreciate the dancing like everyone else."

"We wish we could dance like they can," another of the boys said.

Noah wasn't sure why they were apologising, but he thought it was great that the Year 6 boys wanted to dance like him.

He scanned the room, witnessing the smiles on the faces he saw. This was all except Mr Andrews. He looked angry.

Mrs Rhoda did not allow the Year 6 boys to return to the rest of their class. Instead, they were made to wait at the front as each class exited one by one.

In the playground later that day, Noah and the rest of his dance troupe were joined by numerous other children, all of whom wanted to learn some of their dance moves.

Noah took the lead and tried his best to teach the routine to the other children. Each time one of the children mastered a particularly complicated move or part of the routine, he celebrated it with high fives and his "You did great" dance that he and his dance troupe performed each time they finished a rehearsal.

***

The school's Open Day swiftly arrived. The day had included a series of tours, demonstrations, and discussions, all with the purpose of selling the school to parents of prospective children. The attendees had now begun to fill the school hall in anticipation for the end of day show.

Alex had supported in the set-up of the day, giving his all to ensure he could get the most out of it. He would take everything he learned into his new career.

The end of day show was the moment that Alex had been really looking forward to.

Staff had been asked to adhere to a specific dress code, one that demonstrated the diverse nature of the school. This had resulted in a plethora of colours lining the sides of the hall as the staff members sat either side of the open day attendees.

Mrs Rhoda introduced a variety of musical, theatrical and dance-orientated performances, that demonstrated the freedom with which children were permitted to express themselves at this school.

The Year 4 group were last to appear on stage, a deliberate decision to finish the show with a bang.

Alex had asked Mrs Rhoda if he could arrange a special surprise for this performance to reiterate how tolerant the school was. He also knew that this was a way for him to feel more at peace with his inner conflict. As the Year 4 dance troupe walked towards their starting positions, a number of the teachers rose from their chairs and begun to undo the buttons on their shirts and blouses. After a few seconds, white T-shirts began to appear. These T-shirts were emblazoned with an image of a bee and the words "who you want to be."

Almost in unison the children on stage read the message printed on the T-shirts. Noah mouthed the words, "Bee who you want to be," and smiled at Alex. As the opening beats of the song began, Alex put his thumbs in the air. *This is what I came into this job for.*

As the watching crowd became enthralled with the display on stage, Miss Taylor moved over to Alex.

"You did a good thing," she said.

"Thanks"

"You'll make a fantastic teacher." Miss Taylor held Alex's hand and gave it a gentle squeeze.

Am I ready for someone to know?

"I know by the way," she whispered.

Alex froze. How did she know? He'd been so careful. "You do?"

"Yes, I do. It's okay, I won't tell anyone. That's your story to tell."

Alex kept hold of Miss Taylor's hand until the final seconds of the performance, only releasing it to join in with the rapturous applause that ran through the hall.

It was only a small step. It would be a long time before he'd feel comfortable going into a school and being out from the offset. But it was a start.

It didn't matter if Noah ended up being like him. He just hoped that Noah would be confident enough to express himself on his terms. Alex hadn't had that opportunity, which he supposed was the reason he was so fearful of being found out.

For now though, Alex knew that the next chapter of his life could begin, and maybe he could take the advice he'd given to Noah. Maybe he could be proud of who he was too.

Out At Last
by C.W. Sinclair

On reflection of my life, although it's been a good one, I've made many friends, and travelled to lots of places around the world, it's also been an extremely difficult life. In 1968 I was eighteen and lived next door to my aunt and uncle with my sister, aged thirteen (two sisters had married two brothers). My aunt had a heart condition so Mother had the thankless task of cleaning, shopping, and washing for two households without any of the modern appliances that we take for granted today. My father was a hardworking man, but he smoked and that January, in front of me and Mum, he had a fatal heart attack at forty-six. It is as vivid today as it was all those years ago, has taken me a lifetime to manage, and I still find it extremely difficult to talk about.

I became the man of the house and had to grow up very quickly, in other words to "man up." I would sometimes go to the local pub with my uncle and remember one evening when he quietly said, "Him behind the bar is one of them." I had no idea what he meant and it must've showed on my face because he added, "He's a queer." He went on to explain there were none of "them" around this part of the country—they all live up north—so this barman often went back up north, dressed in women's clothes, and danced around in circles. That was my sex education on "queers." Nowadays it's unthinkable that there could be such a lack of information, but my uncle's bigoted opinion was all I had to go on. And I had to be "the man of the house" so that couldn't be me…could it?

When I was about fifteen I learned a very valuable lesson in life. My friends were always older than myself, and one of them always seemed to get bullied, and I had no idea why. One day he was being picked on, and he tried to walk away, asking me to go with him. To my shame, I refused in case they decided to bully me too. Soon after he and his family moved away. I never saw him again, and some years later, I heard that he'd committed suicide. It turned out that he was gay and life had just got too much for him. I will always remember him, and I have *never* walked away from anyone's side since.

In August of 1999, Mother passed away. I'd always lived with her and couldn't even boil an egg. I was a fifty-year-old man, and this was the first time that I would live alone. Mother would never have been able to accept me as being gay. She loved Danny La Rue though but was convinced he wasn't "one of them queers" and was just acting. I wonder if she would still have watched him had she known he really was gay. But Mother had strong opinions, and male ballet dancers were a different kettle of fish altogether. According to her, they were all "half a woman with something wrong with their brains."

Fast forward to 2009, and I'm a sixty-year-old completely closeted gay man, afraid to come out, fearful of what the family and people would think and say, terrified to bring disgrace to the family. I didn't want to lose everyone's respect. But everything was getting me down. I was doing a job that I hated and felt completely trapped, not knowing what way to turn with my sexuality. I had no one to talk to and certainly no gay friends at all. It felt like I was carrying the cross of Jesus Christ on my shoulders, and every day it got heavier and dragged me further down. I believed myself to be wicked for being gay, and when the day of reckoning came and I stood before the gates, the good shall go to the left but I would go to the right. Hell awaited me. And I was already in a living hell.

That year, whilst travelling in South America, everything got too much for me and I decided to come out to my sister in an email. Her main concern was what other people would think. When I returned home, I took my sister to lunch and hoped to talk about my life, but it never happened. She asked no questions, and I stayed silent.

Another year passed, and I was desperate to make a gay friend. I needed to talk about my life, to make a new life. I was a courier driving for Kodak working ridiculously long hours and I hated it. The stress of the job, my wanting to come out, and other personal problems as well were overwhelming, and I was on the verge of a nervous breakdown. Regardless, I just kept on working and on reflection, I think that job helped to save me because I was too busy to really think about the state of my life.

Eventually, though, I was getting to the end of my tether. I knew something had to change, and I wanted to make some gay friends who I could be myself with. I was trying to figure out how to expand my world and find those friendships without going on dating sites which weren't my cup of tea. I found the Edward Carpenter community online, a gay group who were having a weekend away at Whaley Hall in the Peak district. It sounded like just what I was looking for, so I booked to go. This would be my first encounter with a gay group and I was nervous to say the least. I worried that everyone there would be younger than me and I wouldn't fit in, but I was determined to give it a go.

I arrived on the Friday afternoon and joined nine others. I arrived in the village and drove to a large mansion house that was to be our home for a few nights. It was a lovely building but had seen better days. The group were stood outside waiting for check in, and one guy asked if I was one of them.

"Yes, unfortunately I am," I said. He didn't seem to notice my slip of the tongue, or else was too nice to pull me up on my own homophobia. It was an amazing weekend, and the hall was run by Father John, a gay priest. It was amazing to be myself at long last. We all talked about our lives, and I don't think I stopped talking all weekend. My lifelong shackles fell away, and the weight on my shoulders lifted. I was finally finding the time and space to be myself.

One man had just gone through a very painful divorce,

and another man who came from a religious family was also going through a very painful divorce and had a son on drugs. He was so upset, but there were hugs and unlimited support for him. What a revelation that was! In my world men didn't hug, they gave a good, firm, and distanced handshake. We spent the rest of the weekend walking and socialising, and how I loved being amongst *my* people.

Although the weekend was wonderful, there was no one I particularly clicked with and it didn't lead to any of the lasting friendships I'd hoped for. However, someone there had mentioned the Gay Outdoor Club (GOC), which caught my interest. A walking group sounded right up my street so when I got home I looked it up and joined as a guest member. My weekend away had given me courage, but it only went so far. It dawned on me that the group was local, and that meant I could be seen…and if I was, everyone would know I was "one of them."

It took me ten months to pluck up the courage to go on my first walk with the GOC. I was very nervous, even more so than before going to the Edward Carpenter weekend, but I knew that if I didn't try something new then nothing in my life was going to change. I was still desperate to find friendships with other gay people so I eventually emailed the walk leader in January 2011 to say I was coming along. It turned out to be an amazing day, and I made many new friends.

On that day, my life well and truly started.

There were pub nights and other walks with the group. I came across the East Midlands branch of the group who had camping and hostelling weekends as well. I saw they had an event coming up at Stour Valley in May, and once more, my courage bubbled up enough for me to ring and book it.

It was a lovely hostel in a farm in Constable country, a wonderful walking area. Once again, I made what was to become lifelong friends and was able to simply enjoy being myself. I met one of the group leaders, Sally, and her partner, Fran. Sally and Fran were around my age and had been together for many years. I was glad there were other people my age there; it made me realise that it's never too late to be out and happy. I also found someone that lived in the same town as me, and we became great friends. The weather was great and made for another wonderful weekend. We walked to the mill in Constables' painting, an area unchanged by the hands of time.

In June, I went to a camping weekend in a lovely rural setting by a canal. And though the weather was rather wet, it certainly didn't dampen anyone's enthusiasm. I'd thrown everything into my car rather haphazardly and was struggling to sort things out when two young men arrived. When they opened their car boot—oh my goodness, everything was in neat boxes! They were so well organized and had their tent up and everything done in a flash. Little did I know then what a massive impact Ken and Phil were to have on my life. We bonded during an amazing canalside walk. One couple came in a caravan with an awning and invited us all in after dinner to join them. The drink flowed. It was a wonderful evening though everyone had sore heads the next morning, and we had a mountain of empty bottles to recycle. I suppose it was then I realised that the change in my life was going to be massive.

About a month later I met up with Ken and Phil on a GOC walk, and they told me of their plans to have a civil partnership that October. They asked me to join them, and I felt greatly honoured to share such an intimate event with them after only recently meeting them. I didn't know anyone there, but a lady friend of Ken's came alone. She didn't know anyone either so we spent the day together and had an amazing, unforgettable time.

In 2012 I went with Ken and Phil to Manchester Pride, my first Pride. Wow! The atmosphere was awesome and nearly everyone around me seemed to have a wristband pass for Pride. I couldn't really believe it. It was as if everyone in Manchester was gay. Everything was surreal, and I couldn't believe what I'd been missing out on all these years. The parade was awesome, and that night we went to Canal Street. The crowds, the music, the buzz. It was electric. I loved the crowded bars as I love a good night out and just going with the flow.

Ken and Phil live about thirty miles from me and are over a decade younger than me, but they took me under their wing, and our friendship blossomed. We spent many weekends together at each other's homes, sometimes having parties, and I met lots more friends through the two of them. It was all so different from the many years I'd spent as a closeted gay man and these happy times made me glad I'd found the courage to go along on that first walk.

As my confidence grew, I decided to join as many gay groups as I could. I had a *lot* of lost time to make up. I joined a gay stately homes visiting group, a gay dining group, and an LGBT book and film group. On reflection, it was far too much to take on all at once, especially as I was often helping out the family with childminding around this time. But the groups were all good experiences and a few became important parts of my life.

One of the ones I went to for many years was the book group. We met each month in a backroom of a pub. Every month someone chose an LGBT-themed book, we all read it, and then we talked about it: the usual book club fare. My, we've had some heated debates, but it's all been great fun. I've made some great friends in the monthly gay film group too. I met Zafina at the book group, also her first venture into the gay world, and we've since become great friends who love nothing better than to have a pint or three together and put the world to rights.

I continued to attend the GOC as well, and on a wonderfully hot weekend in August 2013 we had our AGM at Buxton. There were about one hundred and fifty of us, and we took the place over. It was also the Buxton festival, and the campsite and restaurants were packed. Buxton is in a beautiful area, and I went on some lovely walks, and partied hard on the Saturday night in the dome. It was another marvellous memory, and I was determined to build as many of them as I could.

It was on this weekend that I met Barry. Barry is a slim

chap over six feet tall, and he'd cycled many miles to get to Buxton. I only saw and spoke fleetingly to him that weekend, but he would go on to have a huge impact on my life.

Although my social life was going from strength to strength, my family still didn't know I was gay. They would often ask about all the new activities I was doing, and it was getting harder to keep the truth from them. In 2013, I decided to go with the GOC to a private hostel in the Peak District for Christmas. It was a big step as it was only the second time that I'd ever been away from my family at Christmas. They were surprised by my decision. We've always spent Christmas together as a family, going right back to when Mum was alive, and it was difficult to make the break. But the GOC had become my second family and I wanted to spend time with them too. So I went and, despite some guilt, had a great time. The next year I went away for Christmas again, and over time my family adjusted to this new routine. Since then I've come out to them and now they automatically assume that I will be away with the GOC every Christmas. I always have a wonderful time, so I'm glad I made the break.

It wasn't until 2014 that I told my niece and nephews that I was gay. One of my nephew's wives said she'd known when she first met me. So everything was fine. My sister and brother-in-law even came in their motorhome to one of our camping events that year. In December of that year I visited my cousin for her birthday and decided to tell her that I was gay. We sat talking for a while over a coffee and exchanged family gossip. But when I told her, it was as if the wind went completely out of her sails. She slumped down into a chair, seemingly unable to take it in. Some years previous she'd proudly told me that "None of my children can be gay because I've brought them all up the right way." Apparently, being made to "man up" was supposed to make it impossible to be gay. I hoped for a different reaction from her, but I'm not sure why. Hope is a funny thing, especially when it comes to family. When she finally spoke, she told me not to tell anyone. We'd always been extremely close and supported each other through thick and thin, but she made it very clear I wouldn't have her support on this issue. It felt awful when she reacted like that and part of me wondered why I'd bothered to tell her. Things have improved since then and she is more comfortable with it all now, but it's been a long road.

Two more extremely close friends, Alan and Jonathan, came into my life and turned it upside down with new experiences. I'd never travelled first class on a train or flown business class, but they liked the finer things in life and took me to all sorts of wonderful places including trips to Holland and Tenerife. Then, for Jonathan's 50th birthday, he and Alan took a group of us to Sitges in Spain. We started the trip in the first-class lounge at Heathrow airport and from there, it was a non-stop party! We stayed at a boutique hotel opposite the beach with a rooftop pool. There were gay clubs everywhere and the champagne flowed all week. It was an experience I couldn't even have imagined a few years before and would never have gone on by myself. The luxurious surroundings were nice, but it was the company that made it really special. When you're with great friends you always have a good time, whether you're partying in Spain or camping in rainy England.

At Christmas 2015, our group went hostelling in the Peak district and Barry, who I'd first met back in 2013, came along. Barry was a closeted, private gay man whose family knew nothing about him. We'd led a similar life with neither of us having had a gay relationship, we'd been friends for a while, and on that trip, we became a couple. Our friends were thrilled for us, it seemed that they'd known we would get together, and I was so happy to be in my first gay relationship. It was a magical Christmas, neither of us had ever thought we might meet someone to share our lives and experiences with. That Christmas we had some lovely walks in the peaks, fun, and loadsa laughter with our friends —we can be a rather loud group when we're together.

Although Barry and I live about a hundred miles apart and the distance can be very difficult, we were managing, with Barry cycling the hundred miles to me—I did tell you he was a very fit man!

Barry and I love Wales, so I booked two hostels for us. We went to our first one, Rowyn, which is south of Conway. It was an incredibly hard place to find, but eventually we went through a tiny village and made our way up an incredibly steep mountain road. At the top of the tarmac road the hostel was on the left-hand side with a track road going on farther. It had been a small farmhouse, lovely inside, but when we walked to the front, the views were incredible. There were benches to sit on, and the sun was shining down on us. It was just glorious. It's amazing the various people you meet in hostels: an elderly couple arrived who were professors from Cambridge; a man from Russia; and a young lady on holiday from the Philippines. Once again it struck me how wonderful it was to be amongst people from so many different walks of life and still be able to be my true self.

The second hostel was more basic. It was a former farmhouse that had only just had electricity installed, and the water was filtered through a nearby mountain. On our first day there, we decided to take a walk that had been recommended to us to enjoy the fantastic views. Supposedly this was an easy walk of around six miles. Unfortunately, we ended up getting lost in the mountains and repeatedly sinking into the fens! At one point, Barry strode ahead, spotted a river, and announced that he was going skinny dipping. I told him not to even think about it as I was up to my knees in the fens at that point, and he decided against it in the end. What a laugh we had about it all afterwards!

In February 2019, we had a hostelling few days up the Peak District, the weather was wonderful and the hostel was in the village of Eyam, a wonderful place like a small castle. We set off walking the next morning with a packed lunch in our backpacks. The sun was shining, and the clear blue skies were amazing. I hadn't realized it was Valentine's Day and when we stopped in a pub for a drink, there were roses on all the tables. I thought how wonderful it was to be spending this special day with my partner, something I never thought I would get to experience.

One weekend Barry and I visited my nephew and his wife, and their ten-year-old son kept asking why I wasn't married. She finally told him that I was gay. His reply? "Being gay is nothing nowadays, is it?" and he came down to meet Barry. I couldn't help but think how different life is today to when I was young and knew nothing. When homosexuality was a completely taboo subject that nobody ever dared speak of.

When not spending time with Barry, I continued to go on outings and get togethers, including some run through a newly set up local LGBT social group that I'd joined. I enjoyed becoming great friends with everyone and doing many things including playing footy golf (which I hadn't heard of, but what a great evening we had booting a giant ball around a golf course!). I'd never been any good at football and still wasn't. But we all had a great time with the girls trying to teach me.

In May 2019 we had our Northampton Pride with the sun shining. My great friend, Zafina, had an LGBT information stall near the stage, and I stood with her. Lots of friends visited with us during the day. Zafina had arranged for an upstairs room in a bar for us to go to at night, with all proceeds to going to QSpace, an amazing local LGBT youth group. The day and the night were a huge success with everyone having a wonderful time. There were many amazing events last year that I was thrilled to be a part of. One of those was an LGBT book festival organized by two great friends of mine who put an amazing amount of hard work into organizing it. I helped out on the day, selling tickets and welcoming people, and it was wonderful to see some people there who were taking their first step into the LGBT world. It seemed so long ago when that was me. All of the hard work paid off, and it seemed that a great time was had by all.

Life has changed so much for the gay community since I was young, but there are still many challenges today for LGBT people, young and old. It's taken me a lifetime to come out because even though I'm an extrovert, I still found it an extremely scary place to be. There are still some people whom I've known for many, many years that don't know and who have homophobic views, so I don't want them to know. You can't come out to others until you come out to yourself. People tend to think of only young people having issues with their sexuality, but there must be many people out there in my age group, facing the same challenges that I've faced and not knowing which way to turn.

The last nine and a half years have been completely wonderful years. Coming out is a journey, and everyone's journey is different. Coming out is like walking into a deep, dark cavern, stepping into the unknown, and then walking out into bright sunshine. The fantastic friends that I've made and the amount of support given to me has been unbelievable. My journey has been a long and difficult one, and at times, incredibly hard. But as my mother would have said… "There's always light at the end of the tunnel."

Moon Children
by Eleanor Holloway

Only when the clouds coloured pink and the sun was a drop of amber in the sky did Lilith emerge from the safety of her book and the privacy of the woods to offer her help. Baskets of hard little cranberries, crates of rosy apples, and other lovely things. Lilith watched the others migrate them via wheelbarrow and sheer human strength into the centre of the village field, before reluctantly joining in. Piled high, the food formed a pyramid that pointed upward, so Annan, the lady in the moon, could not possibly miss it.

Children played on the enormous round bales of hay, standing wobbly on top and rolling them over until they fell off. Lilith watched with envy as she shoved a crate of pumpkins into the pyramid's bottom.

"Oh, come now. You're far too old to want to play games all day." Her aunt, Eve, raised her eyebrows. "You're a woman now, and you're going to continue growing. Then one day you will be an elder, helping to make all the important decisions for us all."

Decisions? Like choosing the next poor thing to torture to please the invisible woman in the sky? She kept her mouth shut and moved along.

The village elders had been speaking of the great sacrifice, the climax to the evening festivities. Lilith had seen a few in her life: a ram with its throat slit over an oak trunk, twelve chickens thrown from the top of a mountain peak, and a swan plucked naked then tossed into a fire pit still alive and squawking. This year was going to be different. Something bigger. Lilith had only heard whispered rumours and blind guesses, but nevertheless the knot in her stomach tightened with every passing hour.

She approached the group of cousins sitting cross-legged in the herb garden, weaving flower wreaths of red, orange, and yellow. "Has anyone seen Nerissa?"

"Not since this morning." The youngest one shrugged. "Daniel and uncle took her out to the river for eel trapping. Ma says we're not allowed to talk to her. She's still in trouble from yesterday."

Lilith gnawed her thumb with a twitch of guilt.

"Don't look so worried," the middle cousin said and smiled. "Here." She produced a small bunch of lilac bellflowers and delicately tucked them behind Lilith's ear. "There. Now you're pretty."

The eldest, Brigid, said nothing at all. Her eyes stayed glued to her wreath, clearly ignoring Lilith's hard stare. Nerissa's cousins went back to their weaving and began whistling an old tune about frogs hiding in boots. Lilith couldn't help feeling that it was a pointed gesture for her to get back to work.

The trouble yesterday... Nerissa's uncle took care of the sheep and had asked her and Lilith to mark the flock for him. Bored with her other tasks, Lilith immediately set to it, cornering them for five seconds and sloppily striping the ewes' backs with a single, thick black line before they darted away. The sooner she got the job done, the sooner she could return to her precious books.

"Hey! Lilith...look!"

She turned to see Nerissa surrounded by a ring of sheep, with the biggest grin on her face. Nerissa had very straight, very white teeth with long canines that were almost too pointy. If it were not for the smiling that crinkled her eyes and her unrefined, jovial nature, she could easily be mistaken for something less human. Beastly, almost predatory. But Lilith knew her as nothing other than a wonderful friend.

She clapped a hand over her mouth, snorted, and burst out laughing. Nerissa had painted the sheep with bowties and little black jackets, like they were wearing tuxedos. Nerissa had added curly moustaches to some of them. One poor sheep even had big round spectacles ringing its eyes. The herd continued to munch grass, oblivious to their radical new look.

Nerissa's smile widened. Her untameable hair, dark like wet ink, had escaped from its wild braid and was blowing across her cheeks, now darkened pink. Lilith laughed.

Nerissa later shrugged, trying to hide her wince as she limped back to the cottage after her uncle's beating. "Totally worth it. They were going to fly into a rage about something anyway. Might as well give them something good."

A ruby-rich warmth spread in Lilith's chest but was underlined by a twinge at seeing the way Nerissa shakily grabbed the corner of a wall to steady herself. Lilith knew now she should have followed her back, should have told her she didn't need to do stupid things that got her hurt. She didn't need to do them for Lilith, to make her laugh or impress her. Lilith liked Nerissa just the way she was. And she should have asked her to stay the night.

Regret chewed Lilith's brain as she ambled down to her family's bare hut, held together with moss and twine. On village orders, she dug deep into the pantry for the last sack of potatoes. She found a monster of a bag, a lumpy mountain baby, and with great difficulty heaved it out the doorway. It was only a minute's walk back to the field, but her belly turned to water at the stretch of dirt path. Fingers to wrists she was throbbing from chopping wood and peeling pears for pies at the crack of dawn. She knew if she protested too loud, Mother would give her a thumping with her broom.

"Try working faster" was her mother's familiar crow from her hammock under the willow tree. Mother claimed she had to watch the chickens from there, but Lilith deduced such a task was being made less possible by all the empty bottles that littered the grass. Mother would be watching double the chickens they had.

"Try joining in yourself," Lilith muttered under her breath. She gave a hard tug on the bag and heard a dry rip before the potatoes tumbled out onto the dusty floor. Mother's cackle echoed in her ears even when she was far away in the field again.

Night fell. The field filled with the sounds of violins, drums, clapping, and singing. The entire village had come out and formed a circle while they spun their partners around. Nerissa was still nowhere to be seen.

Aunt Eve hissed in Lilith's ear to pass around the dandelion wine and make sure everyone had a drink. Lilith waited until the serving tray was nearly empty before stealing her own mug and slipping out of view. She glanced wildly around the crowd, searching for a glimpse of Nerissa's glimmering, jet black hair. The place was lit up with burning torches that cast a shadowy glow on everything. Twisting, writhing, jumping, ducking, spinning, fire flickered and swam across the silhouettes of villagers.

Out of nowhere, Daniel slammed into her and sent her drink to the ground. He snatched up her wrists and pulled her into a dance. Like his younger sister, he too had ink black hair, but his own teeth were flat little stumps, and his smile was more bulldog than wolfish.

"Follow my rhythm!"

He tugged Lilith towards him, and she banged against his solid chest. Growling, Lilith jerked away, but his grip was vice-like. "Daniel, where the hell is Nerissa?" Her head whirled as he spun her around in a circle in time with the rest of the dancers. Her voice sounded thick, muted above the music. "I haven't seen her since yesterday evening. I'm... getting scared."

Daniel chuckled, and he clenched his ugly jaws. He smelled like a brewery explosion.

"You don't need to be scared, little girl. I'll take good care of you."

He tried to pull her toward him again, but she brought her knee up into his stomach. As he choked out air, she wrenched her hands free from his grasp.

"In your dreams." She turned and ran. She pushed through the dancing bodies, dodged the candlelit table heaving with more wine, fruit tarts, and roast pig, and sprinted down the path to Nerissa's house.

Chest burning, Lilith raced through the dark, grateful for the air cool on her hot face. The cottages were sinister shapes, and the trees spiked like spindly-limbed menaces that crept alongside her vision.

Lilith spotted Nerissa's family home, the last one on the lane. It was the largest in the village, three storeys, with a thatched roof and its own wishing well and dairy house. Hurtling towards the entrance, long sleeves flying, Lilith felt like a banshee coming to terrorise her haunt.

"Nerissa." Lilith burst through the front door. The fireplace was bare. The whole house was pitch black and deathly silent. The thump of her heart was the only echo in her ears as she made her way to the back door. She stepped out into the garden and shivered, despite the sweat running down her arms and her autumn dress heavy on her back.

She scanned the darkness and made out the shape from a hedge: a wrinkled old apple tree....and a cage. Iron, with bars thick as three fingers. Not just any cage, far too big to hold any chickens or birds. Or even a dog.

She saw movement from deep inside the cage. Like a rustle of grass in a breeze or a ripple over a pond, Lilith saw *something*.

"Shit... Is everything okay there? Hello?" Lilith moved closer, cursing herself for not bringing a lantern or even a candle. She squatted down and peered through the bars.

She stilled. "*Nerissa.*"

Nerissa turned around to face her. Lilith easily made out the shape of her heavy brow, her wide cheeks. She could recognise her anywhere. Nerissa opened her mouth but no sound came.

"Do you know where the key is?" Lilith felt panic rising. "How did you get locked in?"

"Oh, I locked myself in here, obviously. I wanted to spend the whole day sitting in a cage."

Even in the dark, Lilith saw Nerissa roll her eyes to the heavens. But she sensed her friend's fear, could taste it like salt in the air.

Nerissa sighed. "No. I don't know where the keys are. As

for the latter, Father gave me my morning tea, same as usual. It tasted weird though, like it was...like..." She frowned. "Never mind. Anyway, I fell asleep. Next thing I know, I've woken up here. High praise to the heavens."

"Right." Breathing in, Lilith swept her hair back from her sticky neck. "I'll go back into the house and find some tools we can use to break the padlock,"

"Yeah..." Nerissa smiled sadly. "Thanks, Lilith."

"Thank me when I get you out of there." Lilith slid her hand through the bars, blindly found Nerissa's, and grasped them firmly, hoping the warmth would bring some comfort. They were linked for a moment, Lilith unsure when to let go. "I'll be quick," she whispered and withdrew her hand. A stinging sensation ached in her palm as she walked away.

Back in the house, she fumbled through the drawer where the family's special box of friction matches was. They were surprisingly easy to use. She lit a candlestick on the table, then began rifling the cupboards for forks, knives, or pins. The sounds of clanging metal filled the kitchen. One peculiar gadget caught her eye. Lilith recognised it as a cake-breaker, used to delicately cut fluffy cakes without crumbling them. It looked like a wide, metal comb with lots of long teeth. She turned it over by its bone handle and smiled. Now it was going to break her friend free.

Lilith gathered up the tools in an empty flour bag and headed back into the garden. As she stepped out again, she thought she heard a creak coming from inside the front of the house but she ignored it and ran over to the cage. "Here."

"You came back?"

"What? Of course!" Lilith set to work. The cage had a roof-like lid with a heavy padlock sat on top. She worked the tooth of a two-pronged fork inside the hole. That was for tension, was it not? Now she needed to stick something else in, and twist...

She found that the cake-breaker was too awkwardly shaped to fit in the padlock and discarded it. She searched around for the knitting needle she'd picked up and gave that a go.

"Lilith...I know I'm probably breaking your concentration but..." Nerissa whispered, "you need to run. Now."

Lilith looked behind her.

Standing before the house were all the village elders, and almost everybody else too. They stood together silently, their lanterns and torch flames flickering in the wind. How had they crept upon her so suddenly and so quiet? An ice-cold claw ran down Lilith's spine.

Lilith stood, gripping the pronged fork tight. "You're monsters. All of you. How dare you treat this girl like an animal? I want her out of this cage, right now." Her lungs scratched like sand; she rarely raised her voice to this extreme.

"Please calm down, Lilith. You still do not fully understand the true intent of tonight," Ivy, one ancient grandmother, said. She inched forward, her long rabbit-fur cape dragging over the wet grass.

"I know exactly what you were planning." Lilith stalked forward in retaliation, heart pounding. "You're holding Nerissa against her will so you can murder her for one of your sickening sacrifices. You'd have to be blind to think this is honouring Annan, as if it's something she would ever accept. All humans are Annan's children, and what you're doing is pure evil."

A male elder next to Ivy raised his head. Brown leaves tangled in his long white beard. "I'm afraid your emotions are clouding your judgement, little one."

"You need to calm down," said Ivy.

Somehow, she had moved closer. Her eyes were blown up huge, rings of gold and fire-red dancing in her swollen iris.

"And besides, I would retract that final statement," she said.

"What are you talking about?" Lilith spared a glance back at Nerissa huddled in her cage.

"Nerissa's family is subject to a very unfortunate curse. It's passed down only through their women, which they are nowadays lucky to be in shortage of."

Lilith sensed Nerissa clenching her teeth, hard. She knew her friend still secretly missed her mother terribly, even if she could not fully remember her.

"It is written in the village almanac that on the first Blood Moon since her first menstruation, the female descendent is to be locked someplace secure and left under the stars to take on her new form, away from the eyes of others. Your friend is no human, Lilith."

Lilith felt her mouth drop, and she peered back at Nerissa who looked just as confused.

"This is the first I'm hearing of it," Nerissa said.

"Indeed, this is a very special night. Two unconnected events, one coincidence. Not only does this Blood Moon occur upon Annan's harvest, but this is the year our almanac declares our biggest sacrifice of all," Ivy said.

Her eyes were sparkling, but her solemn mouth seemed to be fighting off a rising smirk.

"For Annan...we give her a green-eyed virgin."

Nerissa's eyes were coal black.

Lilith backed away as realisation began to dawn.

"So, no, our sacrifice is not Nerissa," Ivy said, leading the crowd closer.

She looked ready to strike, to leap out of that rabbit skin like a pouncing snake.

"It is you, Lilith."

"RUN," Nerissa shouted.

Lilith grabbed her sack of kitchen tools and hurled it straight into Ivy's face, and the old woman went down like a house of cards. The bearded man went for her, and Lilith whacked him with her bag. Another man caught him and helped him stand. Other villagers came charging forward. Lilith whirled around, but someone grabbed her arm and wrenched the bag away. More and more bodies pressed in around her, grabbing at her arms and body until she was forced onto the grass.

Though she screamed and kicked against their pressure, Lilith's hands and arms were bound behind her back, and her legs tied together. Something heavy pressed against her spine, and she realised they were roping some sturdy plank of wood to her, binding her thrice.

Blind terror zipped through Lilith's blood as she was hoisted into the air. Two men carried either end of the plank on their shoulders as the rest of the crowd flanked her sides. Amidst the chaos, Lilith was sure she could hear Nerissa's cries of anguish above the villagers' chants.

As they walked, the villagers started singing an old harvest song, as upbeat as if they were children dancing around a pole in May.

"Lady of the harvest, it is right and meet
That we should lay our first fruits at thy feet
Lowly we prayed and thou didst hear on high,
Didst lift our hearts and change our suppliant cry"

They carried Lilith out of the garden and up through the village. Facing the ground, Lilith could only watch the villagers' shoes, and a few dirty, bare feet. She twisted her head around, desperate to see her surroundings.

The food pyramid loomed in the star-flecked sky. Like a great terrible temple, without the daytime sun to soften its edges, the pile jutted out, imposing its great size and sharpened, uneven corners. The moon had risen to its very peak, only now it was larger, full and ripe, and coloured with a faint blush of crimson.

Still singing, the men planted Lilith's stake high up amongst the crates. She felt the bottom sink down deeper and realised a hole had been dug underneath the pyramid, under all the crates they had spent hours collecting. Nausea gripped her stomach. How long had this been planned? How many people had known, had looked her right in the eyes and silently accepted her fate before she even had the chance?

The villagers' song grew louder, as if to drown out her fear, her struggling against her bonds. Screaming was useless, but all logic had sapped from the universe.

"MOTHER. MOTHER, PLEASE. HELP ME." Lilith stared out into the crowd of faces all around and below

her. But she couldn't spot her mother's unmistakable low-browed scowl nor the bright blue scarf she kept her long golden hair wrapped in. She saw Daniel laughing maniacally, and Aunt Eve waving at her. She was surrounded by people, but Lilith was more alone in the world than she had ever been.

There was a sharp smell in the air, and dark rivulets dripped down over the crates and the pumpkins. Lilith saw the men joining the crowd, having poured foul-smelling fuel over the pyramid. One man moved to hang a wreath over her neck, and Lilith tried to bite his hand. He batted her away and placed it anyway. She might have admired the intricate, woven sunflowers and large blood-red roses under other circumstances.

The man stepped down and continued his song with the village. Was this to go on forever? This gross worship. This taunting.

"We thank thee, Annan,
For all things bright and good,
The seed time, and the harvest,
Our life, our health, our food,
These gifts we have to offer,
For all thy love imparts,
And, what thou most desirest,
Our humble, thankful hearts."

Finally, silence. Three elders came to the front. They had exchanged their usual brown furs for satin robes: one yellow, one orange, and one red. Each of them held a lit tree-branch torch draped in moss, daisies, and little red rowanberries.

"Mother Annan," the elder in yellow called out into the night. "We give to you the treasures of our harvest to relish." She touched her torch to the bottom of the pyramid. It immediately licked up long, amber flames, igniting the chemical-soaked wooden crates.

The second elder in orange stepped forward. "We give to you the sweat, toil, and blood of your children's labour to cherish." He did the same with his torch, adding to the already spreading fire.

Lastly, the elder in red came forward, bearing her branch. It was Ivy, eyes wild in the light of the flames.

"And finally, we give to you our greatest sacrifice. One of our own. As the Menkist almanac tells, a maiden, fresh as a flower with eyes of iridescent jewels and whose soul you shall preserve."

Ivy caught Lilith's eye. Her lips quirked in a smile.

"For all eternity."

Her torch touched the flames of the pyramid. The crowd applauded and cheered as the elders stepped back. The fire rose higher up the pyramid, dangerously close to Lilith's toes. The heat rose quickly and sweat poured from every pore in her body. Her face felt like a mask about to peel away. Her eyes seared, as if they would melt from their sockets like egg yolks, so she shut them tight. The smoke billowed thick and angry, a black fog that encompassed the pyramid and surrounding crowd, choking them.

Lilith tensed and let out one more ear-ripping scream before the smoke entered her throat. This couldn't be how she died. Not now, not like this. Like some farm animal, thrashing in its restraints, its skin sizzling to a crisp, crying out until death finally silenced it.

Screams came from the crowd. Lilith cracked open one eye. Through the smoke, she could see the villagers moving, running away. Something was happening down below.

The red-hot heat reached Lilith's soft shoes, and she shrieked in agony, fighting helplessly against her ropes. Fire was a thousand blades stabbing at once.

Deep, grating growls reverberated at the bottom of the pyramid. Lilith looked down to see the face of a hideous beast staring back, fangs bared. Lilith stopped screaming to draw breath. Would this hell ever end?

Through the fire, the beast scrambled up the pyramid, its huge claws kicking the flaming food crates down onto the crowd. It reached Lilith, its breath hot against her skin. Sweat ran into Lilith's stinging eyes, so she shut them again.

The fire seared through her thin shoes onto her skin.

She felt a shudder, then there was a loud crack. She opened her eyes to see the beast grab at the stake with its jaws, looking as if it was trying to tear it in two. Lilith gritted her teeth, clenched her fists, and willed for this to be over.

But she was lifted into the cool night air, and a blissful whoosh of wind freed her from the agonizing heat. The beast had dragged her out of the fire to lay her down on the grass several feet away from the burning pyre.

Before her brain could form anything coherent, the beast's teeth were at her wrists, tearing through the rope. They felt sharp, and long as the blade of a scythe, but the beast was gentle enough that it didn't bite through her skin.

Soon enough, Lilith was free from her ropes. She rolled over onto the ground, face first into the dewy wet grass, and breathed in deeply.

She heard shouts in the distance and looked up to see the villagers regrouping, perhaps preparing to attack.

The beast nosed at Lilith, poking her armpits. It gave a strange, low whimper like an over-sized dog.

Lilith forced herself to sit up, taking in all of the animal's form. "You...rescued me." Lilith wasn't sure whether to trust her own voice.

The beast was no dog, but it was certainly no wolf either. It was huge, at least as tall as a horse, with a bristling snout full of protruding fangs. It had large, sinewy forearms with wide paws. Upon closer inspection, Lilith saw each paw possessed six long clawed fingers, each as thick as a hammer. As well as a generous bushy tail like a cat's, the beast was covered head to toe in a thick, curly coat of black fur.

Lilith stared at the beast for what must have been only seconds, assessing the new threat. But then its snout was pushing her again, getting her to stand on her feet. She felt weakened as a ragdoll.

"I...I can't," she gasped. "My feet were burned. They hurt."

The beast lowered itself on all fours and turned its head, offering her its back. Grateful, Lilith climbed on and clung to its fur.

The villagers' shouts were getting louder. The bolder of the lot were making their way over, and some of them were carrying axes.

"Get us out of here," she whispered in its ear, but the beast already seemed to know where it was going. It charged straight for the woods surrounding the end of the field. Lilith held on tight, feeling the beast's strong muscles flex beneath its skin as it ran.

The woods were a different world at night. They thundered past blackened trees. Twisted, curved roots were strange, spindly growths in the soil. Lilith enjoyed the wind rushing over her body, cooling her skin. The burning of her toes wasn't as unbearable, but the pain persisted.

Deeper into the woods the beast took them until Lilith was sure they were well clear of the village. The beast had zigzagged, changing direction every few seconds, disorienting Lilith completely. It was unlikely anyone would find them now, especially in the dark. That, and she doubted the farmers' hunting dogs would even be a tidbit of a match for this hulking beast.

Eventually they came to a stop outside the face of a greying cliff. Lilith recognised it as part of the mountain outside the village. "If my memory is right, there's supposed to be some caves around—" The beast jolted and trotted off in the correct direction. Lilith frowned. She had only travelled this far twice before. On both occasions, she and Nerissa had come together. Her chest ached at the memory.

The beast sniffed around and found a cave deep inside the mountain, its entrance hidden by a curtain of mossy vines. It swept them aside with one paw as they entered.

"I... Whoa." Lilith looked around, eyes wide as she adjusted to the darkness. "This is the same cave Nerissa and I found when we had a picnic. That was so long ago."

The beast lowered itself onto the cave floor. Lilith slid off its back and sat against its warm belly. Carefully, she peeled her shoes off her wounded feet, thankful that it was too dark to fully inspect the damage. The thin cloth stuck to the skin of her toes, and she had to pull hard to remove it. The sharp pain made her yell, before her tears fell as she stuffed a fist in her mouth.

She heard snuffles. The beast brought its head in closer, curling around Lilith as she trembled. Its wet tongue dragged across her blistered toes. She stiffened. The warm slobber was surprisingly soothing. Lilith gave her toes a stiff wriggle, and relief unfurled in her chest. She hadn't lost all feeling in them after all.

With a sigh, Lilith settled back into the beast's belly, and pressed her cheek against its fur.

"It's you, isn't it?" she asked into the darkness. "Nerissa." She received another lick, this time across the face. Lilith let out a broken giggle and wiped her nose. "Will you turn back into a human tomorrow, do you think?" Lilith wracked her memory for what she had heard in old legends and fairy tales.

Nerissa flicked her long tail twice against Lilith's leg.

"I guess we'll have to find out, won't we?" Curling up into a ball, Lilith buried her face deeper into Nerissa's fur, exhaustion pressing her to sleep like a heavy thundercloud.

As she listened to Nerissa's heartbeat slowing down, she absent-mindedly picked tree burrs out of her fur. Nerissa's coat, no longer drenched in the scent of woodsmoke and burning fruit, had been cleansed in the fresh, pine-needle scent of the forest.

Just as she was drifting off to sleep, she was sure she heard Nerissa's voice in her head.

"I always thought your eyes were light hazel, not green."

But it might have only been the beginning of a dream.

Illustration by Beth Holloway

Faith and Pride

by *Abigail James*

You will burn.

I let the book fall. It hit the ground without a sound, or at least not one I could hear over the roar that ripped through me. I rushed from the room, my hand clamped over my mouth desperately trying to keep it in, not wanting to free that part of me which was clawing to the surface or wake the toddler napping upstairs.

You will burn.

The bitter taste of sin filled my mouth. I didn't know they said things like that here. I was so used to their "God is Love" stance. This home, which I'd first entered as a member of their church youth group, was full of warmth and kindness, and the hugs that welcomed me were full of unconditional love. So I actually felt welcome. Felt at home. Violent hate didn't belong here. Had I made a mistake, misread the words? No. They were seared inside my mind. They'd scorched my hands as I flipped eagerly to that chapter without consciously knowing why. They had made me drop the book.

You will burn.

I'd never dropped the Book before. No matter how much my scrawny arms had strained to hold it, my hands growing sweaty with the effort as I tried to hold steady so the vicar could read the gospel. He was a giant to me then and I'd struggled to hold it high enough, resting it against my chest. The Book was giant too, with huge print that I followed upside down as I struggled to stay strong. Occasionally he would guide my faltering arms back up, shifting the Book back up my small frame without missing a beat to carry on his painfully slow performance of The Word.

I suspect I managed to hold it there out of sheer willpower. Standing in that central aisle which I had led us down, my determination to play my part and not let them down in the middle of the Sunday congregation. To my right, in our pew two rows from the front, my family would be sat. It wasn't officially reserved, didn't have our name inscribed, but all the regulars knew it was ours. Everyone knew their place. They'd be able to see me clearly from there, see if I slipped.

I never did.

They'd probably call the strength with which I managed to hold on, stubbornness. They might be right.

You will burn.

I managed to breathe, slow my breath so it no longer came in gasps. I sat on the soft sofa in a room away from the library where the book lay there accusingly. I listened for any sound from above to indicate I may have woken Sophie. Nothing. It was tempting to creep upstairs to check, to make sure her sleeping form was still peaceful, and that she had not somehow sensed the fight unfolding beneath her. It was risky though. If I woke her accidentally I'd have to deal with the ear-piercing consequences. How could someone so small cry so loud? It's one of those strange inverse patterns, how we get older and our cries get quieter despite the increased capacity of our lungs. It didn't make sense, but that wasn't unusual. People generally didn't make sense to me. In church there was a script to follow, our words and movements were choreographed precisely, and repeated over and over again. The outside world was not so simple, and there weren't such clear directions.

You will burn.

Sophie and I had a routine for our Saturday afternoons together. I sang and danced her to sleep, a trick I'd developed after it became apparent she made herself stay awake when I was there. She would become increasingly irritable and clingy as she forced her little eyes to stay open, blinking furiously as she kept naptime at bay. If I was there, it was precious playtime where she had me all to herself. I treasured it too. She didn't care about my clumsiness, how I didn't talk the same as others, that I walked on tiptoes and loved to sing. Instead of telling me to be quiet or stop, she would cry out "Again!" We would laugh and play until it was time for me to hold her in my arms and lull her into the sleep she clearly needed. Her mother would tell me how whenever my name was mentioned, she would correct it to "*My* Abby." What mattered was that I was hers.

I *was* hers. She had me wrapped around her little finger from the first moment we met. I'd never really understood that phrase until those tiny digits grasped mine, so unbelievably small yet so strong. I'd been upset when they'd announced her imminent arrival. I'd been afraid that once Teresa had her own child, she wouldn't want me anymore. I was wrong, of course. They had more than enough love to go around. I had become Aunty Abby, one of the army of Godparents made up of the members of their disbanded youth group. And not just that, I was granted a privileged place, more like a big sister. Though the youth group had stopped meeting there after she'd been born, presumably because having a bunch of teenagers around in the evening didn't go well with getting a baby to sleep, I'd been invited back in. *My Abby*. There were other kids I enjoyed looking after, those I babysat when their parents had the occasional night out, and the other toddlers in the church crèche who I entertained at the end of the service who I readily balanced on my hips… but not in the same way. They didn't have the same claim on my heart.

You will burn.

Would they take her from me, this sister who actually loved me? If the Christian youth book that I'd found within their shelves, nestled in that section of their library away from his sci-fi and her romances, was right, would they keep me close and risk getting singed?

I didn't even know why I'd read it. I'd pulled it from the collection when I was browsing quietly as she finally slept, as I did every week. It started with a list of contents, and one entry in particular had caught my eye. *Homosexuality.* It wasn't a word I was used to seeing anywhere, being of that generation who were shielded from knowing all the possibilities of what we could be and who we could love under the long shadow of Section 28. At age fourteen, all I knew was that it wasn't something you spoke about or read about. Except here.

You will burn.

I'd flipped straight to the indicated page, my hands trembling despite the fact this book was only a regular-sized paperback and I was so much bigger now. My arms could hold a child safely by then. I proudly showed off my musician's hands, big enough to reach a whole octave, though when the vicar held them against his, they still looked small and childlike.

You will burn.

I only read the first couple of sentences before the words started to swim before my watering eyes. It was enough. The lesson was clear: homosexuality was a sin and those sinners would burn in hell. Somehow I had felt it was about me, though I didn't know it yet.

You will burn.

I would have to go back in. The book would have to be retrieved and flattened. I prayed there were no creased pages, no sign of what I'd been looking at when it fell. It would need to be pushed back in place, so no one would know I'd abused it. The memory of this moment would need to be pushed back too, buried under thick blankets of denial that would keep it hidden but alive, with those *others*. With the memory of when I'd said to a friend, uncertain and scared, "I think I might be gay" and she'd told me, "Don't worry, you're probably not." And with that memory of when I'd spoken that other whispered word, this time to my mother, a word I wasn't sure the meaning of but that had also hit me with, *is that what I am?* "Don't worry, autism is just a spectrum we're all on. You might be further along it than some people but not as far as others." She was wrong too, but I didn't know better—couldn't know better when no one would explain those things to me properly. So I tried not to worry and to let their false reassurances soothe and lull me for as long as I could.

You will burn.

At least that was clear. There was some peace in knowing for sure: the people who taught me love would *not* love me if I was gay.

***

"I've never met anyone who's gay."

Julia, my manager at the Christian childcare scheme, delivered this statement without any hint she could be joking.

"I'm sure you have, you just didn't know it." Okay, so she may have led a sheltered life but still.

"No, I haven't. I have never met anyone gay," Julia said.

On repetition it sounded even more ridiculous. Could she really believe that? She must've been several years older than me at least, old enough to know better.

"You will have. You just can't always tell." Did she really think we all had rainbow badges and tattoos on our foreheads declaring our sexuality?

"No, I haven't."

"Yes, you have." I wanted to say more, but I noted a colleague looking at me funny, her head tilted to one side as if she was figuring something out. Me. *Shit, did she see me?* I'd forgotten the golden rule again: hide. Hide what you think and hide who you are.

I'd never been much good at that. The truth tripped off my tongue with only the slightest invitation, and it was often a fight to keep it in. Lying didn't come naturally. I didn't like the bitter taste of it in my mouth, though I'd made some progress. It helped if I thought of it like acting rather than dishonesty, and I did like amateur dramatics.

I shifted uncomfortably and went quiet until the subject had safely changed. I still didn't know the law and didn't know that it would be legal for them to fire me based on sexuality because it was a religious organisation. But I still knew better than to out myself there.

I'd only told a few select friends, one simply because she

was my alibi when I attended the LGBT youth centre situated in a nearby town. While I was still living under my family's roof and working with kids under Christian authority, I wasn't planning to change that. But one day, when the house had been empty, I'd found the courage to ring the helpline number and whisper my dreaded secret down the phone. I was counting down the months until I could go to university and finally set myself free. I was just about holding on.

It had got too difficult to completely deny myself, and not just my sexuality. One night I'd attended a Christian youth event at a club and had come home buzzing, determined to engage fully with my faith like the youth missionaries who halted crime with their peaceful presence. I locked myself in my room (barricading the door because we weren't allowed actual locks,) and took out my bible with the aim of reading it cover to cover before I stepped outside again.

I didn't get past Noah. He was how old? It didn't make sense. My brain was just too logical to believe what was in the Book. I couldn't even accept that first story, couldn't understand why Eve was the bad person for seeking knowledge. Surely the one who kept them in ignorance, taunted them, and punished them for learning was the one whose actions should be questioned? I knew most people didn't believe every word, believed context and translations had to be taken into account, but still. It didn't make sense. Blind faith was never going to be my way. I hadn't lost my child's curiosity that had divided my teachers. Some had enjoyed the chance to debate subjects in more depth in an effort to quench my thirst. But others clearly wanted me to shut me up as the sweat beaded on their foreheads with the effort of avoiding my questions, questions they seemed to think were a trick or didn't want to admit they didn't know the answers to.

It'd been easier to stop going to church once we'd moved away from the small town I'd grown up in. We moved less than ten miles to the town where our secondary school was based, but we switched to one of the local churches where no one was particularly invested in me, and I could slip away unnoticed. My brother stopped going too, arguing that you didn't need to go to church to pray. It was factually accurate but not his truth. It was clear he had no interest in praying anywhere.

I couldn't go on pretending, acting like I hadn't lost my faith and that it was no big deal.

It *was* a big deal.

A black hole had opened up inside me where it used to sit. It was a loss that I grieved, alone. I finally told my parents, and their responses made some sense of why they, the intelligent people they were, still attended. My father said that I didn't have to believe everything people had written (like I hadn't already considered that), that I could interpret and believe in my own way and delve into the philosophy he enjoyed. My mother simply responded, "But won't that make life harder?" Maybe. Probably. But just because something was easier didn't mean it was right. Besides, life in the church would not be easy once they knew about me.

As I got older, it became more difficult to keep my head down and not let my differences show. "If you can't say anything nice, then don't say anything at all," and "Nobody likes a smarty pants" could only restrain me so much. Learning to lie had helped, including saying I liked things when I didn't, e.g. boybands, and that I was okay when I wasn't. It wasn't just what I said though, it was the way I said it: speaking so properly even my parents pointed out that I spoke with a suspiciously different accent than my siblings. So I taught myself to swear too. To sound more like other teenagers, I studied a neighbour friend who was excellent at cursing, echoing her as she shouted at the dog to "get the fucking stick." But then people started to say I swore too much.

I couldn't win.

Dating was a disaster. I tried to like boys and copied my friends' schoolgirl crushes, but there was only so much I could fake. At least I had no comparison. I didn't know how wrong it felt until I was first with another woman and that felt so right. I did like some boys, but I didn't like them touching me. My final attempt at a boyfriend ended with a drunken night at an unsupervised house party, though we were thankfully interrupted before it went too far. It was time to ring the support line. I'd had enough of trying to be something I wasn't. They encouraged me to hold on until uni when I'd finally get my chance. *Just hold on.*

In the meantime, I had a job with kids who liked my directness. I didn't bullshit them and they didn't bullshit me. My manager discovered that they would open up to me, like the girl whose dad attempted suicide and the boy who was struggling with his parents' divorce. Neither would talk to anyone else. She said it was a good thing to have someone the kids found so approachable, who heard their truth, though sometimes their truth scared me, and I didn't know what to do with it. Plus, what about my truth? Would she still think that if she knew mine? Would she still trust me? Would their parents? From what I could tell, they brought their kids to us for cheap childcare rather than any religious beliefs. But even if they weren't Christians, it didn't mean they'd want me near their children.

I was less worried about the kids, though their tendency to use gay as an insult bugged me. If they grew up with it being a bad word, how would they be okay with themselves when some of them discovered it applied to them? So I would gently challenge them—no big lectures—and ask them if they knew what it meant, then tell them when they didn't. I used simple words, without judgement, as if it was normal. *Trying* to make it normal, as much for me as for them. Once I'd called out a six-year-old who'd shouted it at one of the girls. His response left me speechless. "Yeah, it means that she was kissing her." He was right, and there was nothing more I felt I could say. Not then, and not there.

***

It hit me as soon as I stepped inside. *Home.* I hadn't got that feeling when I'd visited my parents' house after years of absence, but that could be at least partially because they moved there after I left home, back to the small town and the church I'd been raised in. My mother had always wanted to return, to her friends and her place in that community, and had done so when the youngest of us had finally flown the nest.

My disappearance hadn't gone unnoticed. I had attended church for the occasional Christmas service, my chance to see my church family, but very little otherwise. I was greeted like the prodigal returning, with outstretched arms and tears in their eyes. Teresa, Sophie's mother, held me for so long I didn't know if she'd ever let go. Nothing needed to be said. Even I couldn't mistake their meaning. *Welcome home.*

The vicar did it too, which was a bit odd as I didn't know this stranger who clasped me like her lost child. Apparently, she had counselled and cared for my mother through "everything." God knows what she'd told her. I'd shuddered at the thought and couldn't look her in the eye, which was easy as she stood several inches shorter than me, unlike the gentle giant who towered over me in my childhood. I'd grown tall for a woman: my ex-wife would complain about me putting things out of her reach, forgetting she was much smaller at five foot three.

It wasn't a standard or holiday service that day. I held a new precious bundle in my arms; my darling niece, Priya. There had been questions over whether she would be christened as my brother-in-law, Haroon, was Hindu. In the end, everyone agreed she would go through both rites of passage just like they had multiple wedding ceremonies, that I also wasn't around for. But I was there now, and I hoped to stay.

The service hadn't changed much under the new vicar, and the building even less. The same wooden pews with their individually knitted cushions hung from the backs, ready for us to kneel in prayer, all different patterns and colours that I studied during long sermons. The stained glass still decorated the windows, waiting to come alive when the sun streamed through it at the right angle. I'd admired the luminous scenes as I knelt beside the altar in long robes that had to be tucked carefully to allow me to kneel with my torn jeans and well-worn trainers fully covered, but so I could stand up again without tripping.

As I walked down the aisle towards the altar once more, I tugged at the sleeves of my cardigan to ensure it covered my colourful tattoos and pale scars. Visible scars from my battle with myself. I didn't hide my differences anymore, but I did still hide my pain, and I didn't want to invite any questions. *Don't ask, don't tell.* The altar must've been changed, or had it really only ever been that tall? My childhood vicar used to joke that he would get me a special step so I could reach it, as I struggled to heft the large gold plate containing the collection onto it. Unlike the Book, at least I didn't have to hold it for long, but the loose coins made it more hazardous as there was the risk they could shake free. I never lost a single coin. I didn't need a special step.

As I waited in line, I still hadn't made a decision. My parents were clear I didn't have to join the communion procession and could stay in my seat like a few others, but that would be too clear a rejection. So I had two options: take communion, which I was legitimately eligible to do, having completed my confirmation classes and taken my first communion nearly twenty years before; or I could ask for a blessing instead, like the children and unconfirmed people, those unsure how much to believe or of other faiths. It was all in the gesture I would make as I knelt; hold out my hands for the communion wafer? Or bow my head for the blessing? I reached the front, still unsure. I stepped forward and knelt. On the spur of the moment placed my hands behind my back like Haroon and received a blessing with bowed head and closed eyes. It felt wrong to take the body and blood knowing I didn't believe in it.

After the service, Sophie sat with me at the base of the pulpit, away from the others. The most shocking thing about the day was that she was somehow a full-grown woman. I'd brought her a necklace from my local Christian gift shop to mark her eighteenth birthday. If she was an adult, what did that make me? I'd never been someone to mourn the passing years, but still, I felt...old.

"How am I going to make friends there?" She'd admitted feeling nervous about going off to university in September. "I've lived here all my life and had my friends as long as I can remember."

I was glad she came to me with a topic I knew about, having been not once but twice myself. The first time I abandoned my course when it became clear my real focus was to learn about myself and explore my sexuality, rather than complete a degree. It wasn't a major loss, having chosen what my Grandfather termed a "Mickey Mouse subject." People didn't get why I had, but it was logical to me: why study maths when it came naturally? It was people I needed to learn to understand. My choice of psychology had less noble reasoning behind it too: with lower entry requirements, it took the pressure off as I struggled to make it through my teenage years. Sophie didn't seem to be struggling though, brought up with faith and love and pride.

"There are lots of societies you can join where you can meet people you've got stuff in common with. Go to the freshers' fair. You don't have to stick with the people you live with, or who are on your course. You can find your own crowd." It was something I'd loved about uni, that chance to connect based on what you shared and what you wanted to share. It was where I'd first taken tentative steps from the shadows of secrecy and shame I'd grown up in.

"Okay, thanks. I'll do that."

She still looked nervous. I put an arm around her. "You'll be fine. You'll have an awesome time." She would. She'd grown into a happy, confident young woman who I was sure would have no trouble making friends. My only concern was, had she been too sheltered? Too loved? Would this be her time to rebel?

It wasn't like she was completely sheltered though. She had more idea of the world than I had. I remembered when I'd called Teresa to ask whether it would be okay to ask her to be my bridesmaid for my civil partnership (at that time a new possibility for gays, with marriage not being legal yet), after announcing my engagement and formally coming out in a long letter which had received a positive reply. Before I could finish hedging, she'd called over to Sophie and asked her, both of them sounding delighted. It wasn't the big white wedding I'd imagined as a kid, before I knew or had accepted I was gay, but having her there as my bridesmaid was one childhood dream that had still come true.

***

This was different. My ears perked up as the man at the front of the church started to tell the story of a lesbian human rights advocate, a professor of women's studies.

The sermons there did tend to be less formal than I was used to, the whole services and the venue were too. Instead of carved wooden pews, we sat on fold-up plastic chairs, and instead of holding hymn books, the lyrics of the modern Christian songs were shown on the screens that hung down over the facade of a more traditional church. It seemed you didn't even have to be ordained to lead the services or give a sermon. It was mostly lay people, like this guy. So far he'd been my least favourite of those who took their turn to preach, with his lectures tending to have a distinct whiff of chauvinism to them. So the subject was particularly surprising coming from him.

Except after seeming to extol her virtues, how she worked for education and equal rights, he went on to tell with great joy how she was "saved." She was shown the error of her ways and then left her evil lifestyle to become a vicar's wife and stay home raising his children. Seriously. It was so ridiculous it could've—should've—been a joke. A parody in the vein of *But I'm a Cheerleader*. Except no one was laughing, and the smug smile on his face showed he really was pleased she'd been stopped.

No one else showed signs of anything but agreement with his conclusion. I sat rigid with rage and disgust and fear, my swirling emotions keeping me rooted in place until the very end of his perverse speech. I wanted to run away, but

Steph, the friend I'd come with likely wouldn't appreciate that. Instead I headed for the bathroom. I blasted the tap and splashed the cold water on my face, trying to cool the rage that burned hotter every time I recalled his words and smarmy face, so pleased at the destruction of a woman's life and the end of her good work. Could anyone actually believe that was a better way of life for her? In what sick fairy tale was that her happy ending? Surely I couldn't be alone in seeing through this man's obvious agenda and the misogyny he seemed so proud of.

I stayed as long as I thought I could get away with it and left the sanctity of the cool water when I could hear everyone joining together in song. I should've walked out then, with the clear knowledge that though I may still be welcome in my church, I definitely wasn't everywhere else. Here, I was the enemy that it was their duty to bring to her knees.

I crept back to my place by Steph and sat out the rest of the service still fuming inside. As soon as it ended I turned to her for confirmation of the injustice. "Can you believe that sermon? It sounded like she was doing great before. How can they make out educating on equal rights is a bad thing? Like all women should just stay at home making babies."

"I know."

Her tone was even more hushed than mine, another reminder my beliefs weren't welcome there. I carried on my rant in a furious whisper, paying no mind to the woman who'd quietly positioned herself behind me. "How can they say that love between consenting adults is a sin? Isn't God supposed to be all about love?" It's what I was taught anyway, but I knew not everyone agreed. The youth book that burned me back when I was in my early teens was proof of that. It hadn't stopped me being gay, but it may have helped stop me being religious.

"It is a sin. He's right."

The woman behind us leaned in, and for a moment I was too shocked to speak. I didn't know her well, but I knew she was a powerful woman: a senior member of our police force, not a stay-at-home mum. She clearly didn't follow everything he'd just said, so she was one of the last people I'd expect to enforce his misogynistic view.

"I wish you'd been here when one of our young leaders did his talk, about how he turned away from the sin of homosexuality to God."

She seemed to think somehow that I'd have been willing to sit through such a sermon.

I eyed Steph, but she wouldn't meet my gaze. She was in that service, and I remembered her mentioning one of them spoke about being gay. She'd failed to tell me this was the conclusion. Her betrayal hurt more than theirs, a sharp stab to vulnerable flesh through this gap in my armour. How could she bring me here knowing that?

"We don't believe that we can stop you being gay anymore," the policewoman said.

Well, that was something. I'd had enough therapy, and their brand didn't sound like my idea of fun. I could tell there was a big but coming though.

"But we do believe you can commit not to act on those sinful urges and commit yourself to God, like he has."

She says it like she's offering me an olive branch that I should graciously accept. *Fuck that.* "I don't believe my love is a sin, and I won't try to stop myself loving because of a few suspiciously translated verses in the bible. There are a lot more worthwhile things we can do that will actually make the world a better place."

"No, it's clear. Homosexuality is a sin, if you act on it."

Her voice was full of unwarranted conviction. So that was where she was coming from: *Hate the sin, love the sinner.* Except the people who preached that often seemed to skip the love part.

"You have to commit to a life of chastity if you want to serve God."

She spelled it out as if I simply hadn't understood before. It was clear she had no intention of backing down and neither did I. I wouldn't achieve anything trying to reason with her, but I still gave it a go. It wasn't about the sex, though the idea of giving it up for the rest of my life did leave me cold. I'm a sexual person, I won't deny it, and I don't care for anyone trying to make me. I was done with denial and shame. I'd figured out that was a route to personal hell a long time ago.

I'd like to say that's the last time I went there, that I learned the lesson it wasn't a safe place then. It wasn't. The next time they made me that uncomfortable was when a visiting preacher had them collapsing in a display of mass hysteria (only the women of course, the men were pre-emptively put to work as "catchers,' making it clear how everyone was expected to behave). I *did* walk out that time.

But I think the final straw was when a missionary came to talk about her work. Again, she started off well, talking about working as a doctor and helping build medical facilities in devastated regions. Until she realised what God really wanted her to do was sneak into the houses of Muslim women while their husbands were out to convert them to Christianity, knowing full well that would leave them outcasts in their communities. She admitted she was putting them in danger for the sake of switching to a very similar religion. In my eyes, there was no way a loving God would support that mission over the one she had before.

I was done with their malicious doctrine. If I hadn't experienced anything else, it would've been enough to put me off Christians for good. They weren't saving anyone, but maybe people needed saving from them.

***

I headed down the aisle to the lectern. I wasn't who they were expecting. I was a last-minute substitution. Some of them wouldn't know that, with Christmas being the only time of year that they set foot inside a church. In my family-friendly clothing and with my hair grown out, I probably didn't look out of place to the uneducated eye. Not that those who did know ever made an issue of it there.

The bible was waiting for me, not the one that overwhelmed me as a child, but a more modest affair. We'd checked it beforehand, my dad and I, to ensure there was nothing dodgy that I wouldn't want to read. I'd lend them my voice, the thing I'd learned I most have to offer, but I'd never preach suppression and hate. He'd brought his own preferred version of the Book just in case, which he knew didn't contain anything that would hurt me, in that particular passage at least. It wasn't likely there'd be any homophobia, that really was infrequent. It was the misogyny weaved throughout it that might rear its ugly head. But the reading was inoffensive, chosen to appeal to the masses including those without faith to ease them in gently. I couldn't actually recall any problematic readings or sermons being given there.

I'd reviewed how to introduce and end the reading too, though the refrains I'd recited for years were still firmly planted in my mind. I'd practiced the words to try to ensure I wouldn't stumble, though it was the feeling of being an imposter that would be the cause if I did trip. My dad didn't see my lack of belief in God as an issue, and I still believed in that community. Besides, it was a pleasure to read at a service that wasn't a funeral, the only time I'd performed that duty in recent years.

My dad loves to hear me read, so when he asked me to step up with the accompanying words, "No pressure, feel free to say no," I agreed. He loves watching me act too; we'd even performed together in the Mystery Plays after moving to our new town when I was a teenager. Our audition of Abraham and Isaac brought the other actors to tears. I remembered my disappointment and confusion when the part was given to a boy who couldn't act, no matter how much extra time they spent trying to bring him up to our level. Back here they'd never tried to limit me to the few female roles. They'd laughed and cheered during the family service when I'd thrashed down the aisle as Jonah, engulfed by the whale but not defeated. Funny how my church was one place my perceived gender hadn't mattered. We'd all worn the same robes, and we'd all played the same parts.

My voice shook as I began. Name, chapter, verse. It stilled

as I got into the rhythm of the words, and I managed to keep my pace slow enough for it to boom out clearly. I pushed myself to lift my eyes between verses and connect with the inflated audience. Priya was wriggling in the pew where I'd left her, too young to sit still for long and preferring my lap to the hard seat. It was tempting to bring her with me, her unconditional affection a reassurance, but she would've been too tempted to join in. The Christmas services are family friendly, but they probably wouldn't appreciate a toddler playing with the bendy microphone while the scripture was being read.

I managed it alone, staying in the flow, and offered it up. "This is the word of the Lord."

"Thanks be to God." The congregation accepted my offering.

After, as I moved between the pews, shaking hands and offering peace, hugging those most familiar, Teresa reached for me.

"That was such a wonderful surprise! The best Christmas present!"

From someone else I would've suspected sarcasm, but she sounded passionately sincere as usual. I was happily drawn into her embrace, glad to have given her a gift that had real meaning. The greed of Christmas celebrations got to me, so much extravagance and waste, with people getting into debt buying shit for others they didn't need or even want. It didn't make sense. This felt better. At least it meant something.

I'd never mentioned the book I found at her house. Occasionally I wondered if she'd ever read that chapter, and if she knew what it said. If she did, would she have thrown it away before it could hurt me or anyone else who stumbled upon it? It didn't really matter to me anymore. My mother reported Teresa had boasted how Sophie had marched with Christians At Pride. They told me she'd become known for shaking things up by arguing for gay people to be welcomed in church communities. I like to think growing up with my visible queerness, and her family's continued support of me, helped nudge her in that direction and helped her learn early that there's not just one type of people who deserve to be shown love.

That afternoon, the whole family came around to my parent's house. Teresa had been made Priya's Godmother. She was the obvious choice and always brought her gifts. As well as those with a Christian theme, she always managed to find dolls that weren't white and looked more like Priya than any I'd seen in shops or crèches, dolls that showed her she's lovable just as she is too. I sat back and watched them play and listened to Sophie read to her. She still loved to read, and my toddler niece loved her enthusiasm. People commented on how much Priya looked like me (more than my sister), and it was somehow like our roles had become reversed as Sophie doted on this mini-me.

I snapped photos of them on my phone, capturing Priya's joy as Sophie acted out the parts with fervour. It still didn't feel like home in that house, but it felt okay. It helped that the truce I'd called with my parents appeared to have held. I'd finally sat them down and talked about how we're just different, and maybe we'll never understand each other, but we could accept each other. I wanted to move forward rather than raking over past hurts and conflicts. We'd managed to move on and focus on the things we had in common rather than the things that threatened to keep us apart. I'd come to understand my place in my family and our community, and how I could be with them and be me. I'd gone back to my jobs at the community events run by our church, and I was determined to stick around to be an encouraging influence in Priya's life. To ensure that, unlike me, she'd be raised with pride.

It turned out I did belong there after all.

When they say you just have to find your place in this world, they're wrong. I've found there isn't one place I belong because I'm not just one thing.

It's complicated.

I'm complicated, as are we all.

Maybe not all my parts can fit in one place at one time,

but that's not a problem. I've found different places where I can be different versions of me. I've found freedom in that, in not having to give up on contrasting parts of myself to constrain myself to one role. I don't hide myself, I enjoy being able to let my different selves take centre stage. I am still that child who struggled under the weight of the vicar's bible, determined to earn her place at his side, and I'm so much more. My church family probably know I don't attend regularly anymore, but it's never brought up. Instead we talk about my community work and the charities and marginalised groups I support. We talk about how I spread the message of love they taught me, even though I no longer believe that it's from God.

What's Your Story?

Global Wordsmiths, CIC, provides an all-encompassing service for all writers, ranging from basic proofreading and cover design to development editing, typesetting, and eBook services. A major part of our work is charity and community focused, delivering writing projects to under-served and under-represented groups across Nottinghamshire, giving voice to the voiceless and visibility to the unseen.

To learn more about what we offer, visit: www.globalwords.co.uk

A selection of books by Global Words Press:
Desire, Love, Identity with the National Justice Museum
Aventuras en México: Farmilo Primary School
Life's Whispers: Journeys to the Hospice
Times Past: with The Workhouse, National Trust
World At War: Farmilo Primary School
Times Past: Young at Heart with AGE UK
In Different Shoes: Stories of Trans Lives
Patriotic Voices: Stories of Service

Self-published authors working with Global Wordsmiths:
Addison M Conley
Dee Griffiths and Ali Holah
Emma Nichols
Helena Harte
John Edward Parsons
Karen Klyne
Ray Martin
Robyn Nyx
Simon Smalley
Valden Bush

Other Great Books by Independent Authors

The Copper Scroll by Robyn Nyx
When ambition and romance collide, can Chase and Rayne's love withstand the fallout?
Coming February 2021 via Amazon (ISBN 9781838066833)

LesFic Eclectic Volume Two edited by Robyn Nyx
A Little Something More for Everyone
Download free: https://BookHip.com/FAGAST

Call to Me by Helena Harte
Sometimes the call you least expect is the one you need the most.
Available now from Amazon (ISBN 9781838066802)

Cosa Nostra II by Emma Nichols
Will Maria choose loyalty to the Cosa Nostra or will she risk it all for love?
Available now from Amazon (ISBN 9798690319243)

True Karma by Karen Klyne
Love moves to its own rhythm, if only you stop long enough to hear it.
Available now from Amazon (ISBN 978191644393)

Addie Mae by Addison M Conley
An ugly divorce leads Maggie Carlton back to her hometown, where the chance of a new love comes in a surprising form.
Available now from Amazon (ISBN 9780998029641)

Nights of Lily Ann: Redemption of Carly by L L Shelton
Lily Ann makes women's desires come true as a lesbian escort, but can she help Carly, who is in search of a normal life after becoming blind?
Available now from Amazon (ISBN 9798652694906)

Heatwave by Maggie McIntyre
A quiet weekend in the woods turns into a fight for life.
Available now from Amazon (ISBN 9798550424988)

Printed in Great Britain
by Amazon

65205916R00068